IT Service Management

Foundations

4589651245

IT Service Management

Foundations:

ITIL Study Guide

Author
Ron Palmer, ITIL Service Manager
President, Franklin Technology Strategies, Inc.

Contributing authors
Christine Belaire, Ph.D. LPC, LMFT, NCC
Alex Hernandez, ITIL Service Manager, PMP, CISSP, MBA

Reviewer
Brian Johnson
Member of the original ITIL team and contributor to more than fifteen volumes of best practice in the ITIL space

Forward by Thierry Paquay of Microsoft
Introduction by John Stewart of the OGC

Gulf Stream Press
Corinth, Texas

GULF STREAM PRESS

First printing 2005

ISBN 0-9771469-0-1

Acknowledgments

I would like to thank: Thierry Paquay, for encouraging me to pursue education and experience in ITIL and IT Service Management and for showing me a positive approach to organizational politics; Mark Miller, for helping me study for the ITIL Service Manager exams and for his exceptional people skills; and Manuel Vazquez, for challenging me to expand my organizational agility skills and for encouraging my writing. If not for these three friends, I would not have become an ITIL Service Manager and this book would not exist.

I would like to Thank Alex Hernandez for his contribution in writing a large part of the Security Management chapter and his tenacity and optimism in approaching the University of Dallas with a proposal to offer a graduate program in IT Service Management. This program began in August of 2005 and this book serves as the official course material for the Foundations class.

I would like to thank Christine Belaire, Ph.D. for going over every word of this book and for offering her refined wisdom which helped describe complex concepts in language that is accessible to a wider audience. In her capacity as a communications expert and executive coach, she generously contributed much content that validates assertions in the book.

Brian Johnson, has been an amazing help in confirming my interpretations of the ITIL materials. Brian's perspective, as a member of the original ITIL team and contributor to more than fifteen volumes in the ITIL space, bestows unique qualification. I want to thank Brian for donating so much time and energy to this project, for supporting the University of Dallas Graduate program in IT Service Management, and for introducing me to so many people associated with ITIL.

Sherry Schneider, my friend, advisor, and business partner has helped me in more ways than I can mention. Thanks for your support.

To my wife, Julie, I thank you for enduring the long hours of absence with loving support while I toiled into the wee hours of the night. The strength of our relationship allowed me to focus on the work at hand and I love you dearly.

As my friends and family can attest, writing a book has been my dream for many years. The dream finally came true thanks to many generous people who contributed to my success and the writing of this book.

Thank you all.

48521365

Author's Biography

Ron Palmer born in Shreveport, Louisiana, the eldest of 2 children was later a middle child having gained 2 step-brothers during his teenage years. He "grew up with a keen appreciation for books,"1 was an avid reader, reading everything he could get his hands on! His first influences were of Daniel Boone in early childhood and National Geographic magazines from his Grandfather Keith. His current influencer, no less lofty, is Benjamin Franklin.

Ron's first exposure to hands-on customer service and business operations began at the age of 14 through family run businesses. Ron's mother, Doll, and his stepfather, Tommy, helped to instill a clear sense of how to run family businesses that depend on quality customer service. Throughout the rest of his youth and young adult years, he continued to excel mechanically and creatively challenging himself to find new and better ways of accomplishing objectives. At 17 he successfully completed Marine Corps boot camp and Marine Corps Infantry school. He carries a Bachelor of Arts degree in Information Technology & Economics from Utah State University and holds the ITIL Service Manager certificate.

After leaving Microsoft, where Ron was involved with Microsoft Operations Framework content development and ITIL consulting, Ron founded his own company where he authored an EXIN accredited ITIL Foundations course. He is currently a Senior Partner in charge of content development and training with KEDAR Information Technologies. Ron has been developing, in partnership with other ITIL Service Managers and University of Dallas faculty, the first Graduate program in IT Service Management. Ron's book, *IT Service Management Foundations: ITIL Study Guide* is the first IT Service Management book to be used in this program.

Ron continues to train and consult for Fortune 500 companies while further developing IP in the IT Service Management arena. Ron continues to collaborate with Dr. Christine Belaire, and they have several books in the works.

He takes an active interest in his local city and government and enjoys a beautiful daughter and wife in Corinth, Texas.

Contributing Author's Biography

Photo by Laura Andis

Dr. Christine Belaire provides targeted career guidance to executives, managers, and professionals in all fields who desire to achieve high career goals and recognize that they need focused one-on-one coaching to help them achieve those goals. They recognize the need for objective, specialized coaching to minimize the impact of their weaknesses and to maintain a laser focus on creatively working to their strengths.

Dr. Belaire's professional research and publications focus on communication strategies for achieving a wide range of objectives from business management to helping families build satisfying relationships. She provides these services through her company, Belaire Coaching/Counseling Services. A published author, speaker, and recognized communications expert, she teaches graduate courses at Louisiana State University in the areas of Interpersonal Communications, Career Counseling, and Management of Counseling Services.

Her passion for enhancing relationships through improving communication skills drives her to publish many articles in popular magazines and to write two books simultaneously. The first is a children's book that teaches children to maximize their creative potential, through delightfully funny adventures. The second, a general relationship self-help book, is designed to provide readers with a solid, easily understood foundation for building positive relationships and providing the communication skills to make it happen.

Dr. Belaire is a Licensed Professional Counselor and Licensed Marriage and Family therapist offering a wide range of communication and relationship enhancing services to individuals, couples, and families. Born in Alexandria, Louisiana, Dr. Belaire operates a private practice in Baton Rouge. She holds a Ph.D. in Counselor Education from Mississippi St. University, an M.A. in Counselor Education from Louisiana St. University, and a B.A. in Psychology from Harding University.

Christine Belaire, Ph.D., LPC, LMFT, NCC
Belaire Coaching Services
5233 Superior Dr., Suite C
Baton Rouge, LA 70816
www.BelaireCoaching.com
DrBelaire@BelaireCoaching.com

Foreword

IT Service Management Foundations is a great example of what the popularization and adoption of IT Service Management (ITSM) within IT organizations is beginning to produce; more mature, usable, and practical material toward professional management of IT in large enterprises. Before describing how *Foundations* takes this step forward, I should probably mention that as any self-respecting best practice, the Information Technology Infrastructure Library (ITIL) has room for enhancements both in its core content and in its usability. It continues to evolve as the industry, its users, its training, and its consultancy evolve and require adaptations to newer ways of doing business and of running IT. (For more information on this evolution, please refer to the "ITIL Refresh" results of consultancy report available on the OGC website.)

Of course, *Foundations* does not set out to improve core ITIL content but rather aims to help you learn it. In this endeavor, Ron correctly identifies two key areas where to add value beyond the core ITIL materials:

1. Business context; benefits and justification that provide you with clearer and more practical ties between process-based best practices and business results.
2. Study aids that guide and direct your learning where and when appropriate.

Let's be honest — discussing business context; benefits and justification can be perceived as self-serving, i.e. as a means to convince that ITIL is valuable and should be adopted. I don't think this superficial reading is correct, however. Discarding the business context additions because of this apparent conflict of interest would be a mistake, and here's why: one key characteristic of IT organizations nowadays is their own realization that they exist for business purposes and have to grow out of the legacy mindset of "technology for the sake of technology." This may sound a bit dated, but personal experience working with large and medium-sized Fortune 500 IT organizations around the world has me convinced that this mindset is still solidly anchored deep into IT teams.

The practical result is two-fold: IT managers need to learn to think as business managers or at the very least to interface with their business counterparts in their language. But more importantly, IT managers also need to adopt business methods to improve IT. Business managers have always understood technology for what it is — process automation and enablement. They know that accountabilities, procedures, measurements, organizational structure, reward mechanisms, people, and organizational change management, etc., are required elements to productivity gains, increased sales, quicker time to market, and greater market share.

IT managers are only now beginning to incorporate these realities into their way of managing IT itself. This is no small feat coming from a vendor-dominated environment where any new bit of technology always promises to answer some business need. The recent surge of interest by CIOs and IT leaders in statistical process improvements such as Six Sigma is a telltale sign of their lean toward more business-like approaches to manage. Additionally, a significant lack of benchmarks, case studies, and success stories reveals a need for better integration of best practices for IT Service Management such as ITIL with business management and improvement methods. This I believe makes a good case for the need and even the requirement to integrate IT process best practices with business benefits.

Now for the insightful bit: at a practical level, integration of ITIL and Six Sigma (for instance) requires deep knowledge and understanding of where touch points can be leveraged. The insights discussed in "Defining Success" for change management (pp 99-100) for example would be prime candidates to conduct a Critical-To-Quality (CTQ) analysis and breakdown of measures reflective of the business impact of how IT manages its changes. ITIL V2.0 introduced some of these types of insights and ITIL V3.0 (in early design stages at the time of this writing) will develop this area further. *Foundations* gives you an early look into these thought processes and the ability to step ahead of the learning curve.

The second area where *Foundations* adds to the ITIL text is in the various study aids it provides. For instance, process goals are called out by highlights. If you are studying to take an ITIL test, memorize them! They are the cornerstone of ITIL knowledge required to pass the prestigious Service Manager test and without the ability to quote, dissect, relate, paraphrase, and expand on those process goals, the rest of your study will be extremely arduous and frustrating.

Another example of those study aids are the discussions about the ITIL text which bring deeper and sometimes critical understanding that help make sense of your studying. Ron is not shy about stating his perspective, which although not as authoritative as ITIL itself, (sorry Ron!) is certainly reflective of questions and concerns that you will face when trying to make sense of it all. Learn from those discussions and let them free you to disagree or be critical where things don't make sense.

Even better — get involved in an itSMF Local Interest Group (LIG) as a first step toward contributing your own improvements to ITIL. You will also find sample questions to help you think through your learning and assess your ability to verbalize it in different formats and contexts. Finally, relevant and thought-provoking quotes interspersed throughout the book stimulate your mind and help you "step back" to a higher plane of thinking where you can once again reconcile the fundamental purpose of the best practices: to achieve greater business results.

In conclusion, *Foundations* is a perfect first read for the ITIL student pursuing the ITIL Foundations certificate. Much more than just a study guide, however, *Foundations* also establishes a firm baseline of business context, knowledge, and understanding from which to build your ITSM implementation and consulting skills. As the name "*Service*" implies, I encourage you to think about how you can contribute to this emerging discipline through local interest groups and to truly embrace the mindset behind great service professionals: they love to help others!

Thierry Paquay, Microsoft

Table of Contents

Part II

Part III

Part IV

Table of Figures

1246325498

Preface

All of my life I have been passionate about three things; the act of creating or building things from basic materials; learning and sharing knowledge with others; and organizing activities, things, thoughts, ideas into more desirable arrangements. This book is a unique opportunity to combine all three passions into one project. Creating this book allows me to share what I have learned about IT Service Management with more people than I could ever teach in my courses. The book is organized in a way that makes learning the ITIL concepts required for Foundations certification easy and fun while at the same time providing managers with an informative introduction to its value.

ITIL is the best collection of management best practices and process discipline, applied to technology management, that I have seen. I have enjoyed working with the ITIL materials, teaching courses, and consulting with businesses these past years. I am very happy to be able to share with you my hard won knowledge and experience on this topic. Hopefully, some part of what I have put forth in this book will make your efforts more fruitful.

Welcome to the world of ITIL and IT Service Management. It is my sincere hope that this book gets you started on the journey of continuously improving IT operations capabilities and furthering your career.

Good luck.

Ron B. Palmer

46985325

Part I

FIRST STEPS

485796584

Introduction

IT Service Management (ITSM) is the foundation upon which ITIL builds. It has its roots in the manufacturing quality work of Dr. W. Edwards Deming. The concepts and principles that have worked so well for companies such as Toyota, who have embraced the idea of quality in their products and services, have been adopted and adapted for the needs of today's technology organizations. Companies, such as Toyota, have successfully adapted to increasing complexity in the face of heightened expectations and demanding project schedules. IT management should look to these companies for inspiration and best practices in their own efforts at success.

Although there is much that differs between manufacturing and technology management, there are multiple areas of common ground between them. Most importantly, both are concerned with providing high availability and great functionality at costs that are justifiable for each customer group.

The IT Infrastructure Library (ITIL) is a collection of books that codify many of the best-practices in delivery of IT Service Management. Organized into a framework are eleven specific process areas and one organizational function that serve as a high level model of typical IT infrastructure operations and forms the core of the library.

In the First Steps section of this book, John Stewart, the founder of ITIL, will introduce readers to the IT Infrastructure library, five of the foundation concepts of IT Service Management will be introduced, followed by an overview of ITIL. The information contained in section one will set the stage for understanding the detailed information found in the sections that follow.

7956845

Welcome to the IT Infrastructure Library

Introduction: by John Stewart

It's hard for today's younger people to imagine a time when we didn't have PCs, mobile phones, and the internet. Nowadays, when information and communication technology (ICT) fails, it disrupts business, grounds aircraft, inconveniences citizens, and can even put lives at risk.

The realization, back in the late1980s, that the UK Government was becoming increasingly dependent on IT prompted the Central Computer and Telecommunications Agency (CCTA) to develop the IT Infrastructure Library (ITIL) as a standardized approach to IT service management. The philosophy was to publish the ITIL approach and allow anybody to use it without having to pay a licence fee.

Training companies were encouraged to develop ITIL courses, consultancies and outsourced IT providers were encouraged to offer ITIL-based services. A qualification scheme was established under the British IS Exam Board (an offshoot of the British Computer Society) and later its Dutch equivalent EXIN. A user group, the ITSMF (IT Service Management Forum), was set up.

With all these bodies motivated to promote ITIL-based service management – and thus good quality IT services – a bandwagon started to roll.

ITIL soon acquired an international dimension. Following a CCTA discussion with senior staff in a Dutch company, ITIL became well known in the Netherlands and, from there as much from the UK, took off internationally. Before long the ITIL principles will be embodied in an international standard ISO 20000.

The British Government invested in ITIL because well-managed IT services are necessary for efficient and effective government – in other words, ITIL was developed for the benefit of the UK taxpayer. Companies and governments worldwide are adopting ITIL for essentially the same reasons: good IT service management is good business. And for those who outsource their IT services, ITIL provides some reassurance of quality.

The crusade is far from over. Even now we suffer from business disruption, in the public and commercial sectors alike, caused by ICT faults that effective use of ITIL would have prevented.

Just remind yourself that IT is everywhere in commerce, public administration, and even in many people's private lives. Think what happens when "the network is down." More often than not, business just can't function. People can't work. Customers are frustrated.

Frequently, IT service disruption stems from something the IT department has or hasn't done: poor release management, untested modifications, or ineffective version control. Temporary fixes to faults are hampered by inadequate incident management; permanent resolution is delayed by deficient problem management. Mistakes are repeated because there isn't a system or a culture of continuous improvement.

It needn't – indeed shouldn't - be so. Commerce, government, and individuals have a right to expect boring reliability: IT that is unexceptional because it just works well. ITIL provides us with a basis for boringly reliable IT services.

ITIL isn't rocket science. The concepts are rather simple. In IT service management the challenge for all of us is not to invent something new but to exploit the proven approach that we already have.

I wish you well in your understanding and use of ITIL. It's gratifying that my organization and I have been able to play a part towards the common goals of quality and value-for-money, to which I'm sure we all subscribe. You too have the opportunity to act as ITIL advocates and advance the cause.

John Stewart
Founder of ITIL
Driving force behind its early development.

1

IT Service Management Concepts

Introduction

Quality, not quantity, is my measure.
– Douglas Jerrold

Information Technology Service Management (ITSM) embodies the idea that the IT department is a service organization, delivering IT services to the business. As such, IT should be focused on creating and delivering IT services that provide value to the business. IT Service Management is focused on systematically providing increasingly valuable IT services to business.

To make this idea a reality, IT departments need to focus on these five principles:

- The primary mission of IT is supporting the business.
- Supporting the business means delivering services.
- Effective support results from managing perception and communicaion.
- Consistently good support results from managing to process.
- Long-term success results from delivering quality.

Supporting the Business

Fundamental progress has to do with the reinterpretation of basic ideas.
– Alfred North Whitehead

IT is a mere infant in the business world, having existed no more than a few decades. By contrast, professions such as accounting, production, economics, and marketing have been practiced for thousands of years, with at least three hundred years of well-documented experience to draw upon. For example, Adam Smith published his famous book *"The Wealth of Nations"*[1] *in* 1776, more than two hundred and thirty years ago. Because IT is so new to the business and it has been granted special privileges, much has been tolerated that is not tolerated of the other business professions.

Businesses have allowed IT to communicate in its own language and deliver unreliable, disruptive technology solutions partly because IT is a young organization and partly because those technology solutions were revolutionary. Now, however, technology is going through a period of being more evolutionary than revolutionary, and business tolerance is waning. Businesses have been learning how to incorporate IT into the overall business structure and deciding whether IT is unique enough to require special attention or if it should fall in line with more traditional business professions. The increasing demands of IT from the business are a strong indicator that the latter approach is increasingly being adopted.

What does this mean for IT? It means that IT must move beyond the infant stage and begin to mold its behavior to fit the accepted model. IT must learn how businesses operate and adjust its behavior to fit the larger organizational model. To do that IT must understand the larger organizational model.

The model rests on the premise that businesses exist primarily to generate profit, or in the case of non-profits to fill a stated need. In most cases, IT indirectly contributes to profit generation/need fulfillment, but in other cases, IT is a profit generating activity itself. Even when IT is the primary profit generating activity, it cannot generate that profit by itself.

Why, then, does IT exist? In almost every scenario, IT exists to support the business in its profit generating activities. IT does this by storing and sorting data, by facilitating communications, by speeding up business activities, by improving accuracy and consistency of repetitive activities, and by making possible novel approaches to profit generation. An example of the latter is the ability to order books over the internet from traditional brick and mortar bookstores, which provides purchasers the benefits of both approaches while allowing the business to increase its profitability.

Microsoft Exchange is a classic example of the increasing complexity and interdependent nature of current technology. With the introduction of Exchange 2000 and Windows 2000 Microsoft eliminated a very large duplication of effort. No longer were domain user data and email user data entered and stored separately. With this version, Exchange was given the power to access domain data directly eliminating the need to manage it separately.

From one perspective, this was a significant resource savings, which introduces the potential for even more savings by other technologies. From another perspective, however, it increased complexity, as now the domain services from Windows are critical to the functioning of Exchange and Exchange cannot function if Windows domain services are not installed and working properly. Many companies found that they had to invest significant resources to restructure their windows domain environment just to be able to properly implement Exchange 2000.

IT contributes to a larger business enterprise, which generates profits because it creates a series of processes that are relatively more efficient and effective than its competitor's processes at providing goods and services. Within this enterprise, each entity must identify how it can improve these processes, and its improvements must contribute relatively more value than can be obtained elsewhere. IT contributes value primarily by providing technology services that enable other business entities to increase their contributions. For instance, IT contributes messaging services in the form of email and instant messaging that allows the business to rapidly and effectively share information, which in turn reduces cost and increases productivity.

The value proposition for the business is not a specific email technology. The value proposition is in being able to rapidly and effectively share information. IT adds value not by supplying technology but by supplying a messaging service that provides rapid and effective sharing of information.

For IT to find its rightful place in the business world, it must accept and embrace the idea that IT is a service organization whose primary mission is supporting the business.

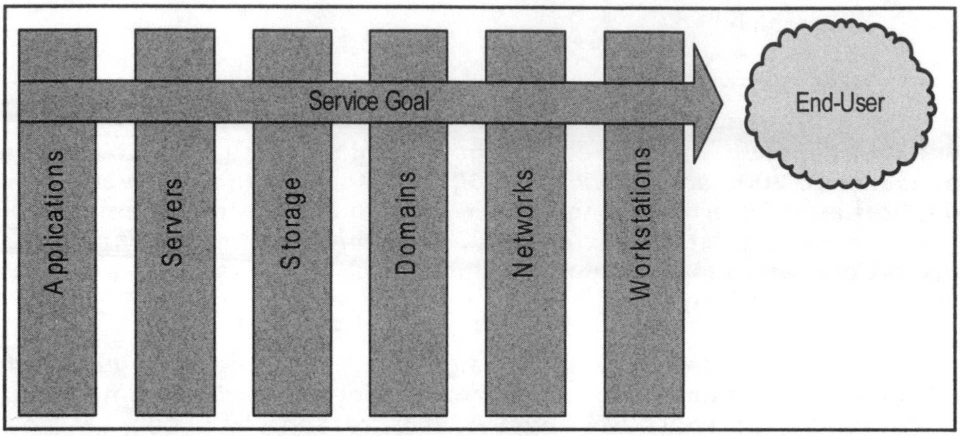

Figure 1-1: Service goal spans silos

Delivering Services

Nothing is more central to an organization's effectiveness than its ability to transmit accurate, relevant, and understandable information among its members. All the advances of organizations – economy of scale, financial, and technical resources, diverse talents, and contracts, are of no practical value if the organization's members are unaware of what other members require of them and why.
– Saul Gellerman

IT has evolved an organizational structure defined by specialization. Technology specialists are typically grouped together with management goals and structure, which are aligned with specific technologies. Even though this type of organization is very effective for ensuring a strong technology focus, it is not very effective for responding to business needs. Natural boundaries arise between these technology "silos" that make it very difficult for the organization as a whole to keep the customers and end-users perspectives in focus. These deficiencies were seldom critical in the early days when technologies mostly stood alone and were not tightly integrated.

Today, technologies are massively interdependent and businesses can no longer function without the aide of interdependent technologies. The drawbacks to technology silos are magnified in this new "enterprise" environment. As technologies become increasingly dependent, communication disconnections between technology silos leads to increasing amounts of unplanned downtime. This is not to say that technology silos should be eliminated. After all, they arose because they provide a significant advantage in deep technical expertise. The challenge then becomes how to keep the deep technical expertise found in silos, while minimizing the communication disconnection that increasingly causes unplanned downtime.

One concept that has proven to be effective in improving communication flows between silos and focusing the organization on customers/end-users is the use of services. How does using services affect communication and focus? The concept of services provides a framework upon which end-user facing goals can be articulated, upon which end-user facing measurements can be collected, upon which communication flows can be mapped, and upon which effective customer negotiations can be conducted.

A commonly used definition of service is: An integrated composite that consists of a number of components, such as management processes, hardware, software, facilities and people that provides a capability to satisfy a stated management need or objective.[2]

Services do not necessarily replace technology silos. They can be overlaid upon the technology silos in a way that maintains the deep technical expertise while focusing activities on supporting the business. This results in a matrix structure where IT staff reports either up the silo management structure with dotted line responsibilities to the service structure or where IT staff report up the service management structure with dotted line responsibilities to the silo structure. This introduces more complexity and management responsibilities, but also improves efficiency and effectiveness, which if implemented well will result in a net reduction in resources required or increased effectiveness while maintaining resource levels.

Some organizations may prefer to eventually restructure around services introducing other organizational measures to ensure that the depth of technical expertise is maintained. The choice is entirely up to the organization and is not dictated by IT Service Management principles.

Why does this work? Managers can normally agree that when management focuses on something and begins to measure it, the organization responds. By defining a goal that focuses on the end-user experience and that provides criteria against which the experience can be measured, management begins to move the organization towards alternate behavior. Focusing on the end-user experience and measuring the end-user experience causes those managers who wish to do well to begin communicating with their peers upon whom their success now depends. It requires them to cooperate in order to achieve a goal that is defined beyond their individual scopes of authority.

This concept can be taken even further by identifying services within IT that are not directly customer facing, but instead, support customer facing services. For instance, Microsoft Exchange 2000 is dependent upon Windows 2000 Domain services. Messaging, provided by the Exchange application, is the service that end-users care about and that customers purchase. Domain services, however, are services that very few end-users ever recognize as being a service, yet they are critical to the messaging services upon which end-users depend. Other services depend upon domain services as well, which means that domain services support multiple IT customers. These end-user facing services provide the desired end-user focus for the domain sub-service. This produces a chain of service delivery that ties the most IT centric technologies to an end-user facing goal.

Focusing IT on delivering services instead of technology serves another valuable purpose, this is to insulate the customer from the underlying technology. By communicating in terms of services, a type of communication the business is already comfortable with; IT frees the business from the need to be overly technology literate. This pays dividends as it frees IT to make technology decisions without being micromanaged by the business. Quite often micro management by the business is a result of the business doing just what IT tried to make it do, become more interested in technology. Business people are experts in their own fields. They should be free to spend their time creating value in their area of expertise not becoming technology experts.

Communication exists for two main purposes: (1) to impart information and (2) to meet needs. Imparting information is a simple form of communication and only requires the transmission of data. However, both the giver and receiver of information must speak the same language in order for the data to be successfully communicated. We rarely miscommunicate the transmission of simple data. However, communicating to meet needs is more complex, and most of our communication mishaps occur from a deficit in this area. Business and departmental communication exists primarily as an attempt to meet the needs of those organizations. However, if an organization has need to satisfy customers then that organization must understand the language of its customers and learn to communicate effectively in that language.

In order for communication to be effective, the message must be both accurately given and accurately received. If either part is missing, then the effort at communication has failed. Effective business communication is a cycle of reaching out and meeting the needs of customers in order to generate revenue. If we are not speaking the same language of our customers or if we do not understand the source of our customer's need because of our communication deficit, then we cannot service the customer and will lose revenue. Imagine trying to conduct

a sales call on a new customer when you each speak a different language and no interpreter is available; it seems an impossible task.

Each business department has a distinct language, and in order for IT to service those departments, it must become multi-lingual. The essence of effective communication is identifying the customer's needs and primary language in order to meet those needs and provide a valued service to that customer.

– Christine Belaire, Ph.D.

Focusing on delivering services has another distinct advantage in that IT customers are already well equipped to purchase services. They regularly purchase all kinds of services from internal and external vendors, and are generally very comfortable with the process. Transitioning IT from a technology provider to a service provider will be a welcome change for the business.

As demonstrated, there are significant gains to be found in moving from a technology focus to a service focus. The focus shift inherently improves communications with customers and end-users, frees IT to do the technology work at which it excels, and frees the business to do the work at which it excels.

Perception and Communication

It all depends on how we look at things and not on how they are in themselves.
– Carl Jung

There is an old adage that says "Perception is reality." Many IT organizations find themselves feeling the sting of reality in these words as IT organizations seem to suffer endlessly from negative perception. Sometimes this is just an unlucky reality, but more often it is the result of IT organizations not understanding some core principles of business and of their own apathy when it comes to self promotion and positive communication. IT service management provides concrete operational activities and tactics for managing perception of two crucial groups, end-users and customers. More importantly, it makes a case for why IT should care more about how it presents itself to the business.

IT in its youthful exuberance has expected the business world to make it the center of attention and to learn its intricate language. This has been tolerated due to the youth of IT, the great benefits of adopting technology, and the inexperience of the business in dealing with this new organization. However, the trend is beginning to change as business leaders become more technologically savvy and as technology becomes more commoditized. Business is beginning to demand that IT conform to more traditional ways of operation.

In its conception, IT asked to be different by communicating only in its language thereby forcing the business to change. Unfortunately for IT, it received just what it asked for and, as a result, IT became micromanaged by the business. One of the unintended consequences of this approach was that business decision makers became emotionally tied to specific technologies, which led them to believe they were better able to make decisions about technology than IT personnel. To counter these unintended consequences, smart IT departments are beginning to abstract technology from business communications by adopting IT service management communication techniques. In short they are communicating in business terms, leaving the complex technical speak for internal IT communications. The result is an independent IT department that is seen as actively supporting business goals.

The primary communication change, speaking in terms of services instead of technologies, is relatively easy to introduce and has significant effects on the way IT operates and in the way business interacts with IT. Some of the key communication elements are:

- IT provides "services" to the business.
- Services are defined in technology agnostic business terms.
- Services are discussed in terms of features, quality, and costs.
- Communications outside of IT utilize either customer or end-user terminology.
- Communications outside of IT focus on the needs and concerns of either customers or end-users.
- Communications internal to IT focus on recognition that IT exists primarily to provide IT services to the business.

Just as teenagers leave behind the casual banter of youth to successfully join the adult working world, so too must IT leave behind its technical jargon if it intends to successfully join the ranks of business professionals. If IT fails to adopt the language of business, it can only expect to be treated as the immature youth its use of language reflects.

Manage to Process

If you can't describe what you are doing as a process, you don't know what you're doing.
– W. Edwards Deming

Process is how business operates. Businesses have processes for building products, for taking orders, for serving customers, and for each and every set of activities they perform. The best companies over time are often those who have the most effective and efficient processes for running their businesses. Processes also ensure consistent delivery of products or services. Process controls provide consistent parameters for operation and a method for assuring stakeholders that the organization will produce acceptable results.

Process is defined as a series of related activities aimed at achieving a set of objectives in a measurable, usually repeatable manner. It defines information inputs and outputs; consumes resources; and is subjected to management controls over time, cost, and quality.[3]

Fast-food restaurants have processes for ensuring that their products look and taste the same regardless of where they are located and that they can be served profitably at very low prices. Regardless of location, the consistent experience, and efficient cost structures are primary sources of profitability for chain restaurants.

IT customers and end-users deserve the same level of consistency and low cost from the services IT provides. Process is the mechanism that delivers consistency of service at low cost. When a business or industry is newly formed, heroic efforts are required by individuals and groups to get the business/industry up and running, and business owners generally recognize that they cannot sustain these efforts over time. Organizational disciplines must be used to ensure repetitive activities are completed quickly, cost effectively, and consistently.

The current practice of treating almost every activity in IT as a one-time activity and relying on heroes to keep the business running is directly responsible for the inconsistent results from IT and the inability to control IT activities. From an end-user perspective, the hero model provides for uneven levels of service; excellent service one day is often followed by non-existent service the next. Customers often have very little confidence that IT can fulfill any of the promises made to the business due to the inherent risk of relying on heroes. There is also an understanding by customers that the hero model is significantly more expensive from an employee cost perspective.

IT is a maturing discipline shifting from heroic effort to organizational discipline. The business is beginning to question the justifications for reliance on a hero model. As a result, IT managers are beginning to appreciate the value of managing to process and are actively pursuing process based management skills.

Why Manage to Process?

Businesses increase profits by creating competitive advantage. IT managers have three primary resources from which they can create competitive advantage people, process, and technology.

IT managers already do everything in their power to hire the best people and deploy the best technologies. They compete in an open market for existing talent and are constrained by competitive realities in how effectively they can attract and retain employees. Competitors within an industry mostly work within the same cost structures. Shifting resources into hiring better staff than its competitors requires permanently taking resources away from other areas.

Likewise, technology is available through an open market. A company's competitors have access to the same technologies at similar prices, and each company can, of course, create its own software. However, this does not create competitive advantage because it requires shifting resources over a long timeframe, it reduces agility, and it can be easily duplicated by competitors.

The Harvard Business Review article, "IT Doesn't Matter," (May 2003, Vol. 81 Issue 5, p41), makes this argument very well. The author makes the case that simply implementing technology in-and-of itself no longer provides competitive advantage to most organizations. Technology has become a necessary cost of doing business, and it provides little if any competitive advantage.

In the rush to keep up with the rapidly moving technology curve, most IT organizations have invested very few resources developing and managing the business processes that support delivery of technology services. As a result, organizations are over spending on people and technology to meet the service levels demanded by the business and living in a continuous reactive fire-fighting state.

Process is the one area that managers have real opportunity to demonstrate value creation and deliver IT driven competitive advantage to the business. Focusing on process requires only marginal shifting of resources on a project basis with real and measurable benefits. As process improvements free up resources, those resources can in turn be utilized on other process improvement projects. In a relatively short period of time, process improvements become self funding allowing IT to continuously improve its service delivery without incurring additional costs.

Additionally, process improvements become unique to organizations and are not easily duplicated by competitors. Even when competitors attempt to duplicate successful processes, they are hampered by incomplete information and the fact that process improvement is cumulative over time. Much like investing, the more that is invested and the longer the investment is allowed to compound the higher the resulting value. Any competitor starting process improvements late will be required to utilize more resources to catch up, weakening them in other areas.

Organizations that invest in improving their process management capabilities often find that they can deliver top quality IT services, while reducing the cost of IT operations. This saving contributes directly to the bottom line or frees resources for use in other competitive areas.

As organizations become more sophisticated in IT process management and build more effective working communications with the business, new methods of leveraging existing technologies are often discovered that give the business a real advantage. These advantages, even if known by competitors, are often difficult or impossible for competitors to duplicate because they require a level of process maturity that competitors have difficulty catching up to. This tends to keep the process based company ahead of the curve and its competitors playing a game of continuous catch up.

A common trap for IT managers is the belief, as demonstrated by their actions, that software can substitute for process. Software applications are critical components in modern business processes, and most businesses could not compete without software applications that automate routine business activities. However, because software automates many of the process activities, it becomes very easy to think that simply installing the right software application will solve all the problems. This trap compounds or shifts the underlying problems. Poorly designed processes end up producing sub-standard outputs faster and more consistently thus magnifying problems in other processes as those outputs become inputs. Problems that were previously fixed by well-meaning employees now become too numerous to fix by the heroic method and often cause significant negative impacts; the source of which goes unrecognized.

It is important for IT managers to realize that technology is only one link in the process chain. To stay competitive, IT managers must begin to help businesses examine the entire process for creating business value and to ensure that the use of technology actually results in increased business value. Only in this way can IT remain relevant and the business remain viable in the face of tough competition.

Deliver Quality

Give them quality. That's the best kind of advertising.
– Milton Snavely Hershey

Quality initiatives in businesses find their roots in the work of Dr. W. Edwards Deming. Business students will recognize Dr. Deming as the person who revolutionized the Japanese auto industry in the 1970s. Dr. Deming was a professor of statistics and was intimately involved in quality efforts for United States war production during WWII. He developed theories about the ability of systems to produce quality and the resultant changes in output quality that occur as changes are made within systems.[4, 5]

Dr. Deming was able to demonstrate with very simple physical experiments that systems naturally reach levels of stability (equilibrium), where the system is producing the maximum level of quality that the system is capable of producing. These experiments show that when a system has reached stability, any attempts to improve quality within the system always results in increased variability of quality. He proved, statistically and experimentally, that the only way to improve quality once a system reaches stability is to change the system.

He created a quality initiative, which proposes that workers tend to produce the maximum quality allowed by the system within which they work. Workers are naturally constrained by the system and rarely have the authority to change it. The authority to change the system rests in the hands of managers. Therefore, the managers hold responsibility for the quality output of the system.

He proposed a system of continuous improvement by which managers with input from workers could improve output quality over time. He developed a very simple PDCA cycle to help companies accomplish this.

- **Plan** – Design or revise business process components to improve results.
- **Do** – Implement the plan and measure its performance.
- **Check** – Assess the measurements and report results to decision makers.
- **Act** – Decide on changes needed to improve the process.

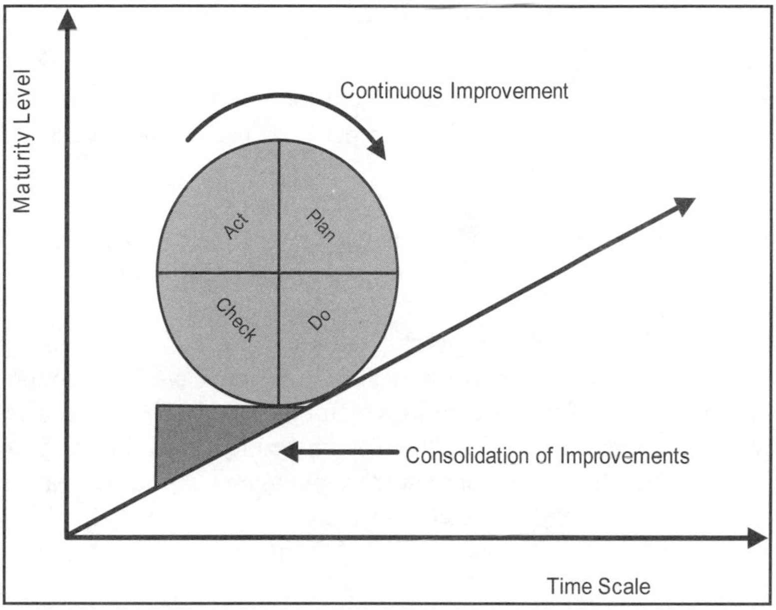

Figure 1-2: PDCA cycle

His theories included extensive use of statistics to measure the level of variability of output for any given system. The goal of his system was to drive out variability.

...the harder they tried to achieve consistency and uniformity, the worse were the effects. The more they tried to shrink variation, the larger it got. They were naturally also interested in cutting costs. When any kind of error, mistake, or accident occurred, they went to work on it to try to correct it. It was a noble aim. There was only one little trouble—their worthy efforts did not work. Things got worse...
– W. Edwards Deming

Today there are a number of well-known quality initiatives that come from this philosophy. You may recognize names such as TQM (Total Quality Management), EFQM (European Foundation for Quality Management), or Six Sigma. The Japanese have even coined the phrase Kaizen for Dr. Deming's continuous improvement philosophy:

> **Kaizen** - the philosophy of continual improvement; that every process can and should be continually evaluated and improved in

> terms of time required, resources used, resultant quality, and other aspects relevant to the process. When applied to the workplace, Kaizen means continuing improvement involving everyone - managers and workers alike.
>
> Kaizen is not limited to manufacturing systems only. It also means continuing improvement in personal life, home life, social life, and working life.

The following quote, written by Claudia Levy for the Washington Post, demonstrates the esteem in which Dr. Deming's work is held at Toyota:

> Since 1951, Japan has yearly awarded prestigious "Deming Prizes" to companies that excel in management and production. Another mark of the esteem in which he is held in Japan can be seen in the main lobby of the Toyota headquarters building in Tokyo. Three portraits dominate the lobby, one of the company's founder, the second of its current board chairman and the third, and largest, of Dr. Deming.

"I'm very impressed by the way the Japanese admire [Deming]," said Gregory Clark, president of Japan's Tama University. "They keep on talking about him as if he's a god."

One of the most impressive demonstrations of the value of this philosophy is the success of a Japanese company that was little known in the early 1970s in the west. Today it has surpassed Ford as the second largest producer of automobiles in the world second only to General Motors. In 2002, Toyota was third worldwide in automobile production behind General Motors and Ford. That year it earned a net income per unit sold of $1,022 compared to General Motors's loss of $17 and Ford's loss of $141 per unit sold.

The following graphs illustrate the net income per unit for the major auto makers of the world over the period from 1995 to 2002[6]. Figure 1-3 shows the actual numbers for each year. Note that Toyota, in red, shows a consistent year after year growth with net income per unit almost doubling over this period. As demonstrated in Figure 1-4, the only company doing better than Toyota is Honda, which is another quality focused company that employs Dr. Deming's ideas.

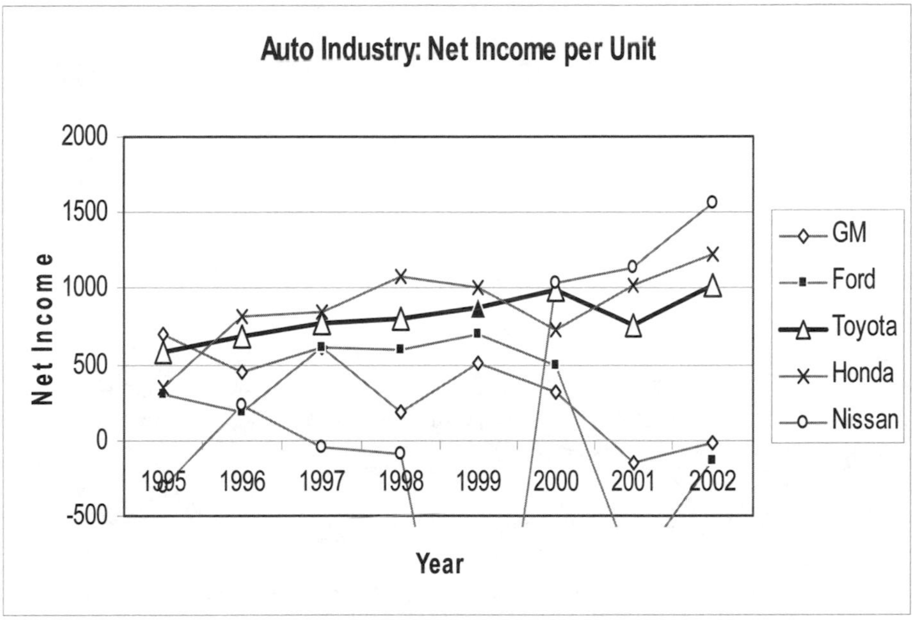

Figure 1-3: Net income per unit

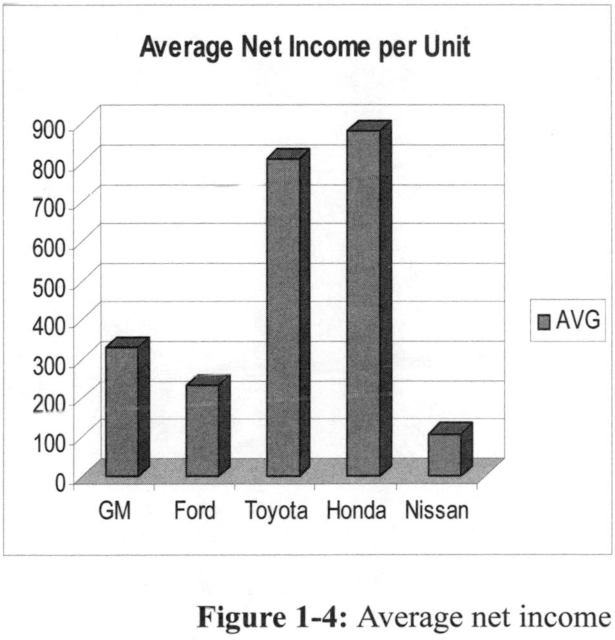

In this graph average net income per unit over the same 8-year time period is dramatically higher for the two Deming companies. Their average more than doubles that of their closest US competitor

Figure 1-4: Average net income per unit

Just as Japanese companies have adapted and adopted Dr. Deming's recommendations to fit their cultural requirements, IT needs to adapt and adopt his recommendations to fit IT requirements. Fortunately, a very good effort has been made to do just that. This effort is codified in the books that make up the IT Infrastructure Library (ITIL). The remainder of this book will introduce ITIL and the operational, tactical, and security processes codified in the three ITIL books titled *Best Practice for Service Support* (operational), *Best Practice for Service Delivery* (tactical), and *Best Practice for Security Management.*

Conclusion

This chapter focuses on five key principles to introduce students to the concept of IT Service Management.

- The primary mission of IT is supporting the business.
- Supporting the business means delivering services.
- Effective support results from managing perception and communication.
- Consistently good support results from managing to process.
- Long-term success results from delivering quality.

These concepts if applied with care and understanding will form the basis for a highly competitive IT organization that contributes meaningfully and recognizably to business success. Those organizations that choose to ignore such sound principles are likely to find themselves in reactive mode constantly playing catch up with their competitors or with outsourcers.

1 Smith, Adam, *The wealth of Nations*, 1776

2 *IT Service Management Terms, Acronyms and Abbreviations*, Version 1, (North America, 2001, ISBN 0-9524706-6-7

3 *IT Service Management Terms, Acronyms and Abbreviations*, Version 1, North America, 2001, ISBN 0-9524706-6-7

4 *"Dr. Deming: The American Who Taught the Japanese about Quality,"* By Rafael Aguayo, 1990, ISBN 0-671-74621-9

5 Liker, Jeffrey K., *The Toyota Way: 14 Management Principles From the Worlds Greatest Manufacturer,* McGraw Hill, New Yourk, New York, 2004, ISBN 0-07-139231-9

6 International Trade Administration/US Depart. of Commerce, Automobile Net Income Data charts, <http://www.ita.doc.gov/td/auto/finwebjan2004prelim.pdf>, accessed on December 2004.

2

IT Infrastructure Library

Introduction

Warning – Customers are perishable.
– Store Sign

The IT Infrastructure Library, a collection of best practices in IT service management created in the late 1980s by the CCTA (a British government body, now absorbed within the Office of Government Commerce (OGC)), is the *de facto* standard for IT Service Management. Version 2 (latest revision) evolved into a framework of processes and best practice activities and has been updated to reflect the current state of technology management. It is available to the general public under an open copyright, which allows others to utilize the information and is supported by many well-respected companies.

What exactly is ITIL and how can it be used? ITIL is a set of books that describe methods for managing technology in a business or nonprofit environment. These methods form a system that is based on the quality work made famous by Dr. W. Edwards Deming which has spawned systems such as Six Sigma, Total Quality Management (TQM), Lean Production, the Toyota Production System (TPS), and others. ITIL differs from these systems in that it is specifically designed to apply this valuable knowledge directly to the provision of IT services. The best practice, quality methods have been specifically adapted to meet the unique challenges of delivering IT services. It can be used by any IT organization to improve delivery of IT services on a continuous basis.

ITIL is designed to be usable by organizations of any size and structure. Its guidance is applicable to companies with only one technology manager as well as the largest government organizations, which may have thousands of managers. The material is designed with the expectation that companies will adapt and adopt the specific guidance that is applicable to their organizations, and that companies thoroughly understand and document why they deviate from its recommendations, when they do so. It is not designed to be a standard enforced by a governing body, but simply a framework of best practice examples to follow. Documenting deviations simply allows for organizational learning and organizational understanding of why a non-best practice path was followed.

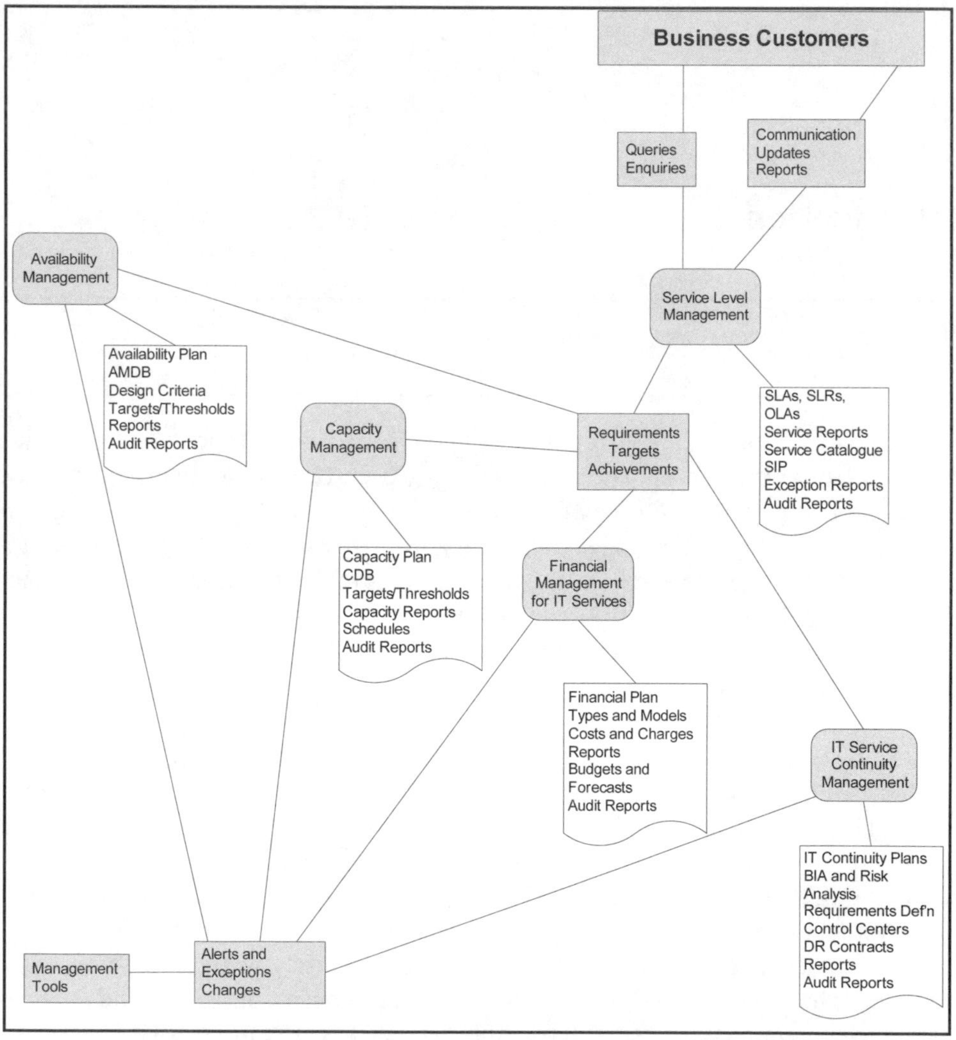

Figure 2-1: Service Delivery process model

The British Standards Institute (BSI) and the International Standards Organization (ISO) have, in the case of BSI, already adopted standards derived from the ITIL materials (BS 15000); or as in the case of ISO are actively working on a standard derived from the ITIL materials (ISO 20000). These standards can be used by organizations to show that they have complied with the published standard much as companies currently comply with the ISO 9000 standard.

Since its publication, many organizations have adopted ITIL guidance and demonstrated significant value, in the form of cost savings and competitive advantage, from its application.

There is also a healthy market of consulting and training companies that specialize in helping the business world adopt and adapt ITIL for their unique situations.

ITIL as a framework describes a model for organizing the management of IT service delivery. This aspect of ITIL provides some predictive capabilities in that changes in one area can be shown to affect other areas through process inputs, outputs, and communication flows. Further, ITIL, as best practice, provides specific actionable recommendations for improving service delivery that typically do not require drastic changes. In other words, ITIL guidance can be implemented in small manageable chunks without the need to "rip and replace" entire management structures. This provides for incremental improvements and manageable projects that show definitive returns.

ITIL does not suggest a "rip and replace" strategy for process improvement. Instead, the best practice nature of the content allows for selective application of ITIL guidance. The framework aspect provides insight into how selectively changing one part of IT might affect the whole of IT service delivery. In essence, targeted service management changes can improve the overall quality of service with minimal investment while the framework provides understanding of the larger systemic changes to which these incremental changes lead. The systemic changes will unleash the value of leverage between process areas, the area of maximum benefit from ITIL.

Philosophy

There is really no insurmountable barrier save your own inherent weakness of purpose.
– Ralph Waldo Emerson

Since ITIL was created by the British government, it is written in British English, and there are many subtle differences between British English and American English. For instance, the term ethos, commonly used in British English, is not a common term in American English. In American English, the equivalent of ethos is philosophy. Below is an excerpt from the preface of the ITIL Service Support book. All of the ideas and concepts expressed in this ethos will be discussed throughout the book.

> *The ethos behind the development of the IT Infrastructure Library (ITIL) is the recognition that organizations are increasingly dependent upon IT to satisfy their corporate aims and meet their business needs. This growing dependency leads to growing needs for quality IT services - quality that is matched to business needs and user requirements as they emerge.*
>
> *This is true no matter what type or size of organization, be it national government, a multinational conglomerate, a decentralized office with either a local or centralized IT provision, an outsourced service provider, or a single office environment with one person providing IT support. In each case there is the requirement to provide an economical service that is reliable, consistent and of the highest quality.*
>
> *IT Service Management is concerned with delivering and supporting IT services that are appropriate to the business requirements of the organization. ITIL provides a comprehensive, consistent and coherent set of best practices for IT Service Management processes, promoting a quality approach to achieving business effectiveness and efficiency in the use of information systems. ITIL processes are intended to be implemented so that they underpin but do not dictate the business processes of an organization. IT service providers will be striving to improve the quality of the service, but at the same time they will be trying to reduce the costs or, at a minimum, maintain costs at the current level.*
>
> *For each of the processes described in this book, one or more roles are identified for carrying out the functions and activities*

required. It should be noted that organizations may allocate more than one role to an individual within the organization (although this book indicates where specific roles should not be merged), or may allocate more than one individual to a role. The purpose of the role is to locate responsibility rather than to create an organizational structure.

The best practice processes described in this book both support and are supported by the British Standards Institution's Code of Practice for IT Service Management (PD0005), and in turn underpin the ISO quality standard ISO9000.

Organizations

The purpose of an organization is to enable common men to do uncommon things.
– Peter Drucker

There are different types of organizations that play roles in the creation and adoption of ITIL. This book will discuss four types of organization:

1. The creator and owner of ITIL
2. The certification bodies
3. The international user group
4. Third party training and consulting companies

OGC

The Office of Government Commerce (OGC) is the British government agency responsible for creating and distributing ITIL. ITIL was originally created by the Central Computer and Telecommunications Agency (CCTA), which has been absorbed by the OGC.

EXIN & ISEB

These agencies are nonprofit certification bodies which are authorized by OGC to issue ITIL certifications, set requirements for certifications, and to certify training companies. They also provide certifications and services in other areas such as PRINCE2 and CMM. From a certification perspective, it makes no difference which agency issues the certification. Certifications issued by one are accepted by the other and both are accredited by OGC. These agencies work closely with the OGC to define a common set of criteria by which to certify individuals and training companies.

If you take the ITIL Foundations exam and pass, you will receive an ITIL Foundations certificate from either EXIN or ISEB.

EXIN stands for the Examination Institute for Information Science and is described as follows on their website.

> *EXIN, the global IT examination provider is an independent organization establishing educational requirements, and developing and organizing examinations in the field of Information Technology. EXIN is well-known worldwide for its ITIL certificates in IT Service Management. With examinations like ITIL, ISPL, CMM, ASL and DSDM, EXIN plays an important role in the development of international qualification standards.*[1]
> *http://www.exin-exams.com*

ISEB stands for Information Systems Examination Board and is described as follows on their website.

> *ISEB qualifications add value to professional careers by providing both the means and the platform for recognition and enhanced career development.*
> *Through the Information Systems Examinations Board or ISEB, BCS provide industry-recognized qualifications that measure competence, ability and performance in many areas of IS, with the aim of raising industry standards, promoting career development and providing competitive edge for employers.*[2]
> *http://www.bcs.org/BCS/Products/Qualifications/ISEB/*

itSMF

The IT Service Management Forum (itSMF) is an international professional users group. The United States hosts an active chapter and has an annual conference for IT Service Management professionals; it also produces books and provides professional resources.

The itSMF is described as follows on their website.

> *The IT Service Management Forum (itSMF) is the only internationally recognized and independent organization dedicated to IT Service Management. It is a not-for-profit organization, wholly owned, and principally operated, by its membership. The itSMF is a major influence on, and contributor to, industry "best prac-*

1. Paragraph taken from the EXIN website March 2005, http://www.exin-exams.com
2. Paragraph taken from the BCS website March 2005, http://www.bcs.org/BCS/Products/Qualifications/ISEB/

tice" and Standards worldwide, working in partnership with a wide range of governmental and standards bodies worldwide.[1] *http://www.itsmf.com/*

ITIL Training and Consulting Companies

There are a number of companies in the industry offering ITIL and IT service management training and consulting. Accreditation for ITIL training is provided by EXIN and ISEB to companies only, not individuals. Course materials are created by the training company and must be submitted to and reviewed by the accreditation agency as part of the accreditation process.

Companies are accredited by exam type (see certification below) so a vendor can have accreditation to deliver ITIL Foundations training and not IT Service Manager Training (commonly referred to as ITIL Masters). There is a sequence to the accreditation process. Companies must first be accredited to teach ITIL Foundations for a set period before they can become accredited to teach the IT Service Manager course. Typically, vendors must be accredited to deliver ITIL Service Manager training before they can become accredited to deliver Practitioner training.

There are no certification bodies recognized by OGC or itSMF that provide certification of ITIL implementation knowledge, ITIL software compliance or similar IT service management consultant certifications. Anyone can claim to be an ITIL consultant regardless of qualification or experience. It is recommended that anyone seeking ITIL consultants ask for proof of training certification from the consultants. Consultants should have at a minimum the ITIL Foundations certification and be directed by an ITIL Service Manager (commonly referred to as an ITIL Master). They should also be able to demonstrate intellectual property (IP) that shows they have experience in the field. In other words they should be able to demonstrate supporting materials in the form of documentation, guidance, templates, graphics, and process/procedure documentation to support the claim that they are experienced consultants in this field.

---

1. Paragraph taken from the itSMF website March 2005, http://www.itsmf.com/

Books

Books constitute capital. A library book lasts as long as a house, for hundreds of years. It is not, then, an article of mere consumption but fairly of capital, and often in the case of professional men, setting out in life, it is their only capital.
– Thomas Jefferson

The ITIL body of knowledge, represented in a collection of eight books, is widely accepted as the leading source of IT service management guidance. These books are created by the OGC and can be obtained from the Stationery Office website www.tso.co.uk. The title and a brief description of each book are provided here:

1. *Service Support* documents the five operational process areas and the Service Desk function. IT represents the operational foundation upon which business value is created. The process areas are:
   - Service Desk (The function)
   - Incident Management
   - Problem Management
   - Change Management
   - Release Management
   - Configuration Management

2. *Service delivery* documents the five tactical process areas. It takes the outputs from the operational processes and begins the transformation of IT activities into strategic business value. The process areas are:
   - Service Level Management
   - Financial Management for IT Services
   - Availability Management
   - Capacity Management
   - IT Service Continuity Management

3. *Planning to Implement Service Management* documents a process-based approach to implementing and improving processes.

4. *ICT Infrastructure Management* documents planning, delivery, and management of quality IT services for business users of IT in the areas of Network service management, operations management, management of local processors, computer installation and acceptance, and systems management.

5. *Application Management* documents planning, delivery, and management of quality IT services for business users of IT in the areas of the software devel-

opment lifecycle and business change, specifically requirement definitions and implementation.

6. *Security Management* documents how to organize and maintain IT infrastructure security from the IT manager's point of view.

7. *Software Asset Management* documents how to effectively manage, control, and protect software assets through all lifecycle stages.

8. *Business Perspective: The IS view on Delivering Services to the Business* documents how IT managers can align IT activities to the needs of the business.

The ITIL Foundations exam is designed to test a student's foundation level knowledge of the material covered in these three ITIL books; *Service Support*, *Service Delivery*, and *Security Management*. The exam is provided by either EXIN or ISEB through one of two means; a proctor provided by EXIN or ISEB may deliver the test following a course, or the student may take the exam at a Thomson/Prometric testing center.

This book is designed to provide students with a fundamental appreciation of the elements of service management primarily as described in the ITIL books *Service Support*, *Service Delivery*, and *Security Management*. It should also provide the student with sufficient understanding of ITIL to pass the ITIL Foundations exam.[1]

Certification

Learning is like rowing upstream; not to advance is to drop back.
– Chinese Proverb

There are three types of certification for the ITIL materials (Foundation, Practitioner, Service Manager) representing two different certification tracks (Practitioner and Service Manager). Each track requires the student to have achieved the ITIL Foundations Certification before moving to the next level. The Foundation exam consists of 40 multiple-choice questions, and students have 60 minutes in which to complete it.

1. Sample exams are provided, for an additional fee, at the following website www.GulfStreamPress/Foundations/.

There is a governing board, the International ITIL Certification Management Board (ICMB), with representation from the OGC, EXIN, ISEB, and the itSMF that determines the requirements for students to be allowed to take each of the exams. Although it is recommended that students attend the two-to-three day course associated with the foundation certification, students are permitted to self-study for the certification exam. However, for both the practitioner exams and the Service Manager exams, the governing board requires that students attend an accredited course before being permitted to take the exam.

The ITIL Practitioner track is in transition as of the writing of this book. It is transitioning from tests associated with each process area to tests associated with four cluster areas. One of the cluster areas (IPRC) is available as of this writing. The second cluster (IPSR) will be available no later than July 1, 2006. The four clusters and the primary information covered are:

1. ITIL Practitioner Release and Control (IPRC):

    - Managing IT changes and releases
    - Providing configuration information
    - Configuration control
    - Change Management
    - Release Management
    - Configuration Management

2. ITIL Practitioner Support and Restore (IPSR):

    - Service Desk
    - Incident Management
    - Problem Management
    - Primary end-user liaison
    - Incident resolution
    - Problem solutions

3. ITIL Practitioner Agree and Define (IPAD):

    - Creating service levels
    - Agreements with customers
    - Managing contracts and SLAs
    - Planning and managing cost and revenues
    - Service Level Management
    - Financial Management for IT Services

4. ITIL Practitioner Plan and Improve (IPPI):

- Planning availability
- Planning capacity
- Planning IT service continuity
- Availability Management
- Capacity Management
- IT Service Continuity Management

The ITIL Practitioner track is for those individuals who only need the complete depth of understanding for one or more process areas. As an example, a service desk manager needs in-depth understanding of three areas: Service Desk, Incident Management, and Problem Management. Individuals involved primarily with Change Management need in-depth understanding of three areas: Change Management, Release Management, and Configuration Management.

Under the old scheme these individuals would need to attend one to five days of training and would achieve a practitioner certificate for each process area covered, in contrast to the service manager track which is ten or more days of training. Both the practitioner track and the service manager track cover the material to the same depth, the difference is that the practitioner track allows the student to concentrate on a select subset of process areas only.

The Practitioner course typically runs one or two days per process area. The individual exams consist of 40 multiple choice questions, and students have 120 minutes in which to complete each one.

Under the new scheme these individuals will take a five-day course covering the information listed under each cluster. The course will include practical assignments that must be completed before sitting for the exam. There is one exam per cluster that contains 40 multiple choice questions and allows 120 minutes for completion

For those who will be involved in IT service management across multiple process areas, the IT Service Manager track is appropriate. This track guides students through an in-depth understanding of all of the process areas and their relationships to one another. There are two scenario based essay exams for this certification consisting of five questions each. One test covers the *Service Support* materials and the other covers the *Service Delivery* materials.

Conclusion

This chapter provides an overview of the IT Infrastructure Library (ITIL), its history, design criteria, the philosophy behind its design, the organizations supporting ITIL, the books that make up its guidance and the certification structures provided. This information is included because it is required as part of the accredited course work and it gives students a framework of understanding of the chapters that follow. The chapters that follow will cover the Service Desk function and the 11 process areas upon which the certifications are based. These 12 items are documented in the three ITIL books *Best Practice for Service Support, Best Practice for Service Delivery,* and *Best Practice for Security Management.*

Part II

SERVICE SUPPORT

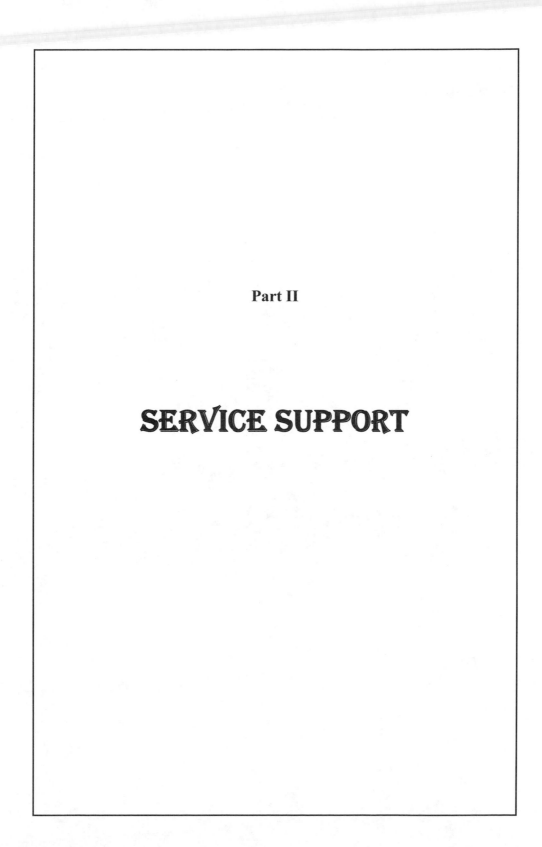

Introduction

Section II covers the ITIL book *Best Practice for Service Support,* or the "blue book." It is a collection of the five operational processes and one business function:

1. Incident Management
2. Problem Management
3. Change Management
4. Release Management
5. Configuration Management
6. Service Desk

These processes are considered operational in nature because their outputs are consumed by either end-users or internal IT processes such as the tactical processes discussed in *Best Practice for Service Delivery.* These processes are the inner workings of IT and are the bedrock upon which business alignment rests. These processes must operate effectively and efficiently and be designed to collect appropriate data consistently if the tactical processes are to provide business aligned services.

Many organizations want to jump directly into the visibly high value service delivery processes without first doing the hard work of optimizing the service support processes. Organizations that attempt this approach quickly realize that there are many critical dependencies that are not met under current operating conditions. Therefore, jumping directly into service delivery processes typically fails to deliver value.

Just as any athlete, artist, or professional can attest, superstars only become superstars after they have mastered the basics. Those who do not may have moments of glory that represent just a flash in the pan. The one-hit wonders and long forgotten heroes are those who ignored the basics. Organizations must operate on a continuous basis, and there is no room for one-hit wonders in a continuing business operation.

Take the time to master these operational processes: (1) learn and react appropriately to the differences between end-users and customers, (2) understand why process goals and critical success factors are important, (3) explore how so many benefits come from simply separating incidents from problems. These concepts are the basics of ITIL and of Service Management. In-and-of themselves, these things are small. However, just as basic blocking and tackling is crucial to winning in the American game of football, the basics of Service Support are crucial to winning in the business of enterprise IT.

Throughout this section the terms Configuration Item (CI) and Configuration Management Database (CMDB) will be used. They will be defined and discussed in detail in the last chapter of this section titled Configuration Management. The reason these topics are defined in the last chapter is that they are difficult concepts to grasp without first seeing how and where they are used. For now, consider a CI to be a component in a database or a decision support system that represents the lowest level of granularity tracked as an item in the IT infrastructure. The CMDB can be thought of as an IT decision support system that collects data from all the different data stores in the enterprise then relates and displays that data to decision makers in the form most useful to making better decisions.

3

Service Desk

Introduction

Unless you have 100% customer satisfaction...you must improve.
– Horst Schulz

In ITIL the Service Desk is considered to be a function, not a process, and it does more than simply log and resolve incidents. Although Incident Management and Service Desk are intimately connected, the Service Desk has a larger role as it handles more than just incidents. The Service Desk in ITIL is a front-end function for change requests, service requests, complaints, queries, and any other needs that end-users have of IT. Some organizations take this concept even further by utilizing the Service Desk as a central point of access for all internal business services.

Highly efficient and effective Service Desks separate their activities into at least two major categories: call routing and technical support. Routing of calls is a strictly nontechnical activity that takes a significant amount of time in the aggregate. Therefore, it becomes beneficial to any organization of significant size to allocate nontechnical staff to route calls, based on carefully prepared procedures and scripts.

Once a call routing group of this type is created it becomes very economical to have them route all requests for internal business services. The business efficiencies to be gained become significant in aggregate. Every member of the organization then has one number and/or email

address to remember to gain rapid access to any internal service. The time savings alone in simply locating the correct contact person for a service can significantly affect organizational productivity. Service response times often improve, and service providers no longer duplicate this activity, resulting in more effective use of time and technical resources.

In this way, highly specialized and trained call routers can collect all the required information for the appropriate record i.e. incident, Request for Change (RFC), service request, move request, maintenance request, security request, etc. Once this vital part of the process is completed, the record and the call are transferred to the appropriate service organization (i.e. Technical Support, Change Management, Facilities, etc.).

This level of detail is inferred but not documented in the ITIL materials. It is provided here as an example of the value to be earned by implementing ITIL best practices.

There is a very good reason to have a single and consistent face to the end-user community. End-user perception is a critical element of the business' determination of how well IT performs its job. As such, it is important that IT do everything practical to ensure that end-users enjoy a consistent and professional experience when interacting with IT.

The best way to achieve this is to simplify and consolidate the points of contact between IT and the end-user community. ITIL (and many other best practice frameworks) recommend that Service Desk be the single point of contact between end-users and IT. This means, that at the very least, IT provides a single phone number and email address utilizing Service Desk principles and call routers to provide end-user access to IT services.

The concept of a Service Desk differs from the traditional concepts of a call center or a help desk. It is important to understand the differences from an ITIL point of view. A call center differs from a Service Desk in that the call center is mainly concerned with handling large call volumes for telesales services, where the Service Desk has much larger responsibilities. A help desk differs from a Service Desk in that the help desk is primarily concerned with handling incidents and is not a single point of contact for end-users, nor does it manage the complete range of requests, as does the Service Desk.

Given that many organizations do not embrace the Service Desk concept, ITIL suggests that an awareness campaign be organized to educate leaders about the benefits of embracing the concept. Some of the benefits identified by ITIL for implementing a Service Desk function are:

- Increased accessibility to IT for end-users

- Better quality and speedier turnaround of end-user requests
- Improved teamwork and communication
- Enhanced focus and a proactive approach to service provision
- A reduced negative business impact
- Better managed infrastructure and control.
- Improved usage of IT support resources and increased productivity of business personnel
- More meaningful management information for decision support

Goal of the Service Desk

The goal of the service desk is to:

- Act as the central point of contact between the user and IT service management.
- Handle incidents and requests.
- Provide an interface for other activities such as changes, problems, configuration, releases, service level, and IT Service Continuity Management.

For every need that an end-user has of IT, there should be an acceptable response from the Service Desk. For every IT activity that affects an end-user's ability to work, there should be proactive communication from the Service Desk, explaining what to expect. Service Desk should act as the single point of contact for end-user interaction with IT. As such, Service Desk is primarily responsible for the perception of IT by end-users. If a company is experiencing end-user dissatisfaction with IT, then the Service Desk is the first place to look for answers.

Clear delineation of goals and responsibilities is one of the ways in which ITIL improves efficiency and effectiveness. The value of this distinction is best illustrated by showing how the responsibilities of Service Desk, Incident Management, and Problem Management differ. Contrary to typical help desk operation, the Service Desk in ITIL is not concerned with identifying the root or underlying causes of incidents. Root cause identification is the responsibility of Problem Management and is conducted only in response to a problem record. In contrast, rapid restoration of service is the responsibility of Incident Management. When the Service Desk processes incidents, it is acting as a front end for Incident Management and is therefore concerned with rapid restoration of service only. This distinction will be further discussed in the Incident Management and Problem Management chapters.

Many organizations have difficulty utilizing reports from their help desks to effectively improve service delivery. Part of the problem is the lack of distinction between incident records and problem records. Without clearly identifying the differences and collecting detailed information separately for each, it is very difficult to identify precisely how and where resources can be allocated to improve the process.

Customers vs. End-Users

Everything should be made as simple as possible, but not simpler
– Albert Einstein

To this point, the terms *customer* and *end-user* have been used without discussion of the differences. We are all familiar with the idea of a customer from the consumer point of view where customers purchase and consume goods and services primarily with their own money. In this scenario, the customer and the end-user are one and the same; however, in an enterprise environment this relationship is more complicated.

In the enterprise environment, there are many end-users but only a few customers. End-users consume or utilize the services that IT provides, while customers purchase those services. Customers have budget authority or political influence sufficient that they obtain services from IT for a group of end-users. In the enterprise environment, customers and end-users are distinct groups with differing needs and drivers.

Recognition of these differences has impact on IT's ability to manage perception and to communicate effectively. Customers have concerns for things such as value for money, cost of services, business value, etc. End-users are typically concerned with functionality, reliability, ease of use, Service Desk responsiveness, etc. Tailoring communications and services for each group improves business perception of IT making it easier for IT to get the resources and commitments it needs.

A great storyteller tells stories the same way regardless of the audience-right? Wrong. Great story tellers are great communicators and understand that each audience is different requiring a unique performance. In our everyday interactions, we utilize this principle regularly. When we are speaking to a child, we change our voice tone and pitch, we simplify words, and use exaggerated expressions. Similarly in social situations, we may alter our language to accommodate the particular listener or receiver of the information. For example, when

speaking to a minister, most people will curb their use of foul language; or when speaking to an English teacher, they will intentionally use proper grammar (even when they don't normally). Further, men and women frequently speak differently to one another than to each other. Men have a language that they use only with men, and women speak to women in their own language. When they communicate across genders, they change their communication strategies.

The concept of adapting our language to suit the recipient is common, but we somehow fail to generalize it beyond 'special situations' where we deem it necessary. We assume that when adults speak to one another, they all understand and interpret communications in the same way.

Effective communication, however, always considers the perspective and goals of the receiver of the communication. It is the communicator's responsibility to know the audience and to adapt his/her language to that audience. Mediocre storytellers force their audiences to adapt to them. Great storytellers deliver a unique experience to every audience.

From an IT perspective, the two primary recipients of communication are customers and end-users, each having distinct needs and goals. Furthermore, each of these groups has specific communication needs based on their professional affiliation or their place in the organization. If IT is to effectively manage satisfaction, it must learn to distinguish between its intended recipients and tailor communication to each group.

– Christine Belaire, Ph.D.

Even though *Service Support* and *Service Delivery* introduce these concepts in section 1.8 of each book, the remaining chapters of the books use the terms very loosely. The terms may also be used loosely in the exams. Therefore, while this best practice is valuable to implement in your organization, do not expect precision of language in either the ITIL books or the ITIL exams.

Service Desk Functions

We evaluate the services that anyone renders to us according to the value he puts on them, not according to the value they have for us.
– Friedrich Nietzsche

The Service Desk has many functions; the most important of which is overseeing restoration of normal services in support of Service Level Agreements. It is also concerned with functions such as collecting information about incidents, logging Requests For Change (RFC), and facilitating all communication from IT to end-users. As the owner of incidents and the primary interface with end-users, the Service Desk is responsible for monitoring incidents and problems and keeping end-users informed of their status. This is done within the process parameters provided by Incident Management and Problem Management.

Students should be aware of the common Service Desk functions identified by ITIL:

- Receiving calls, first-line customer liaison
- Recording and tracking incidents and complaints
- Keeping customers informed on request status and progress
- Making an initial assessment of requests, attempting to resolve them or refer them to someone who can resolve them based on agreed service levels
- Monitoring and escalation procedures relative to the appropriate service level agreement (SLA)
- Managing the request life cycle, including closure and verification
- Communicating planned and short-term changes of service levels to customers
- Coordinating second-line and third-party support groups
- Providing management information and recommendations for service improvement
- Identifying problems
- Highlighting customer training and educational needs
- Closing incidents and confirming with the customer
- Contributing to problem identification

Every request that comes into the Service Desk should be recorded even if the request is inappropriate for the Service Desk to handle.[1] This ensures that IT

---

1. Inappropriate requests occur primarily when the ITIL Service Desk concept is not fully implemented. If a user contacts the Service Desk when they should have contacted some other group, it may indicate that training or communication needs to be improved.

management has the information needed to improve service provision. As an example, if inappropriate requests have reached a significant level, it indicates that management action (i.e. end-user training) is required. If the inappropriate requests are not recorded, management is unable to recognize that the number of inappropriate requests has become significant. Likewise, requests that take less time to resolve than to record should also be recorded. Even though it is not always apparent to the person recording the request, every request is a source of information for improving service delivery and may be needed by other process areas.

Types of Service Desk Structure

If the shopper feels like it was poor service, then it was poor service. We are in the customer perception business.
– Mark Perrault

There are three types of Service Desk structure identified by ITIL:

- Local Service Desk
- Central Service Desk
- Virtual Service Desk

The local service desk is a service desk that is very close to the end-users. Therefore, large organizations will have multiple local service desks each with redundant staffing and costs as well as probable inconsistencies in delivery. This type of service desk is fine for small organizations but introduces additional costs as the organization grows.

As organizations grow, they begin to recognize the costs associated with multiple local service desks and often over react. The tendency is to centralize all service desk functions into one large centrally located group. If the organization is itself centralized then this type of structure is a logical solution. However, if the organization is distributed then the centralized service desk will likely result in reduced quality of service as support staff are remote from many end-users.

Fortunately, technology has provided a solution that provides centralized control while allowing resources to be placed close to end-users. The current state of networking and telecommunications technology allows resources to be distributed to almost any place on the globe that is desirable for the organization. This technology allows for centralizing some resources where centralization makes sense and distributing others where that makes sense; for instance, distributing resources to locations where labor costs are relatively lower (i.e. off-shoring). The newer technology allows for use of consolidated systems for these distributed resources, which reduces duplication of effort and wasted resources

Another option opened up by technology is the idea of follow-the-sun support, which means having the primary response centers shift from region to region with daylight hours so that the staff works normal business hours in their region while supporting global operations, thus lowering the need for overtime expenses and 24-hour staffing in every region. Telecommunications and networking technology allow for phone numbers to be rerouted when one center closes and another opens and for utilization of the same software tools regardless of location. For large multinational companies with capable organizations this option has many benefits.

End-User Communication

In business you get what you want by giving other people what they want.
– Alice MacDougall

As the central point of contact for end-users, all communications with end-users should be directed through the Service Desk. This provides an authorized source of information for end-users that is not dependent on end-users recognizing particular IT staff. For instance, email from IT to end-users should all come from a Service Desk alias so that end-users recognize it as official information from the IT organization.

Expectation management is often a simple tool to implement and one that pays great dividends. Everyone who utilizes a service will come to that service with her own expectations for what constitutes great, good, or bad service. That expectation is determined by her previous experiences with other similar services.

One problem IT faces is that end-users have expectations that are often divorced from cost considerations. IT and customers determine agreed service levels based on the cost of providing service and the existing budget constraints. End-users are often unaware of the service level targets that are agreed and rarely aware of the costs, leaving the Service Desk in the unenviable position of meeting undefined and differing expectations from end-user to end-user. How can the Service Desk get control of this situation?

The answer is to set expectations early in the conversation by tactfully presenting the agreed service level targets to the end-users. One scenario where this technique is very effectively used and that almost all of us have experienced is with pizza delivery. When a customer calls

for pizza delivery, they are usually given an expected time of delivery of anywhere from twenty to forty-five minutes. By presetting the expectation in this way, the pizza delivery service has clearly established the goal by which they are to be measured. That goal is agreed by both parties, and it is one on which the pizza delivery service can deliver. In this scenario, everyone is happy when the pizza is delivered in the agreed time frame, even if the customer originally wanted a twenty-minute delivery.

The example scripts presented here utilize this simple concept to both communicate agreed service targets and to document them for both parties, setting expectations at the bar established between IT and the customer and gives the end-user the opportunity to object to the agreed service targets, which might result in renewed negotiation between IT and the customer.

Much of the routine communication from the Service Desk to end-users can be automated. This ensures end-user confidence that the process is performing as expected and provides end-users with an opportunity to correct any inaccuracies or miscommunications. This section provides three examples of automated communication that can be leveraged to initiate or improve the automated communication process.

The incident confirmation receipt informs end-users that their incident has been officially logged into the incident tracking system and will be assigned to a technical resource for resolution. Notification should accompany every incident, even if the incident is resolved immediately, letting the end-user know that the information is formally tracked and managed. It puts a professional face on IT and contributes directly to positive end-user perception of IT and indirectly to positive customer perception of IT.

Some key points to note from this document and the others that follow:

- The language is clear and business oriented.
- Technical language is minimized or eliminated.
- Assignment of a reference number assures the end-user that the incident is being formally tracked and is unlikely to fall through the cracks.
- Expectations for response times are set by the Service Desk in line with SLA targets. This is an indication that end-user expectation is being actively managed.
- The problem description is clear and in end-user accessible language.
- Contact information is identified, allowing the end-user to proactively identify inaccurate data, minimizing the opportunity for missed service calls.
- The expected method for end-user follow up is clearly identified.

Incident Confirmation Receipt

Dear Mr. Smith,

We are pleased to inform you that your reported incident has been added into the service desk tracking system. Your assigned reference number is **INC-22323**. This number should be retained for reference purposes. A support analyst will contact you before **Monday 12-Jan at 12:00 hrs**.

Reference No. **INC-22323**

Description: Laser Printer not working

User Name: Mr. William Smith
Location: Library Rm.34B
Telephone: 555 - 1234 ext. 2322
Mail address: Smith_W@EVE21

Expected completion by: **Monday 12-Jan at 17:00 hrs**

Should there be any further questions or queries, please do not hesitate to contact the service desk at 555-2345. Please have your assigned Reference Number handy.

Yours sincerely,

John Jiles

(Service Support Specialist)

Installation confirmation informs the end-users that their request has been assigned to someone for resolution and tells them when they can expect resolution to take place (expectation management). In this instance, a new computer has been requested and approved. This request has been formally logged into a request tracking system and is being professionally managed.

The installation confirmation below is an example of functional escalation, where the incident (in this case a service request) is something that the Service Desk is not equipped to resolve. The appropriate action for the Service Desk is to:

- Record the details of the service request.
- Create a service request number.
- Notify the end-user that someone will contact them within an agreed time frame (SLA determined.)

- Retain ownership of the service request, but escalate to appropriate support group.
- Monitor the service request and keep the end-user informed of the status.

Installation Confirmation

Dear Mr. Smith,

We are pleased to inform you that your installation has now been scheduled. Your assigned Reference number is **SR-22325**. This number should be retained for reference purposes

Description: Installation of New PC

Location: Library Rm.34B
Telephone: 555 1234 ext. 2322
Mail address: jansen_w@eve21

Start Date: Tuesday 14-Jan 2000 at 09:00
Expected completion by: **Wednesday 15-Jan 2000 at 12:00**

Should there be any further questions or queries, please do not hesitate to contact the service desk at 555 2345. please have your assigned Reference Number handy.

Yours sincerely,

Jill Adams

(Service Support Installation Manager)

Some reasons for the Service Desk to escalate incidents are:

Sometimes the impact of an incident on the business grows over time. For instance, often an incident has little or no immediate real impact on the business as end-users can utilize their time effectively while the incident is being resolved. However, over time as the incident remains unresolved, dependencies or deadlines become increasingly important. In this case, the incident would need to be escalated to more senior resources and/or brought to management attention.

SLAs contain service targets that IT is expected to meet. In order to ensure that these targets are met, IT establishes triggers and thresholds that require escalation of incidents within sufficient time to allow more senior resources and/or management to respond before the targets are missed.

Every organization has political considerations that must be accounted for. Sometimes incidents may have little or no real impact on the business, but may get a high level of negative attention because of a perceived political impact. In order to ensure that political considerations are managed at the appropriate level, incidents are often escalated.

The service support confirmation receipt informs end-users that their request or incident has been attended to and that the Service Desk is requesting confirmation that the issue has been resolved to the end-user's satisfaction. Notice that the terminology used is in plain "NON-IT" language

Service Support Confirmation Receipt

Dear Mr. Jansen,

A support specialist has been in attendance to your Incident. Reference Number:INC-23323

Incident corrected: Yes [ ] No [ ]
Date/Time: Monday 12-Jan 2000 at 09:20
Reported Symptom: unable to print
Solution: replaced faulty printer cable

Should there be any further questions or queries, please do not hesitate to contact the ACME Service Desk at (214) 555 - 1313. quoting your assigned Reference Number.

Keep in mind that Service Desk is a service function, and as such, customer service (end-user) best practices should be observed at all times. IT personnel should never talk down to an end-user. End-users are professionals in their own fields and deserve respect. The Service Desk should, at all times, use language that is respectful and appropriate to the technical understanding of end-users.

It is also important to request that the end-user indicate if the incident has been resolved satisfactorily or not. Sometimes IT may believe that the incident is resolved, but the end-user may still be unable to complete the task. Often this identifies a need for training or one-on-one assistance for the end-user. If the Service Desk assumes the incident is corrected without confirming with the end-user, there is a high likelihood that the end-user will be dissatisfied with the service provided by IT. Furthermore, that end-user may find an alternate means to meet their needs, and the Service Desk will never know that an unsatisfied customer has been created. It only takes a few such customers for IT to gain a very negative reputation.

Pre-Release Requirements

Quality in a service or product is not what you put into it. It is what the client or customer gets out of it.
– Peter Drucker

Every organization should prepare a standard pre-release checklist that should be reviewed prior to major releases by the Service Desk Manager, Change Manager, Release Manager, and the Service Level Manager. Any release that affects Service Level Requirements should be rolled out only when Service Desk has everything it needs to ensure those service level requirements can be met.

Service Desk has activities to perform following any major change or release. To accomplish these activities effectively and efficiently, Service Desk requires specific information from Change and Release Management prior to the completion of any major change. Some of the requirements ITIL identifies are:

- An up-to-date service catalogue
- Up-to-date processes, procedures, and documentation
- Training of Service Desk staff to the required level, including training on any technology support tools being used (Service Desk tools, email, knowledge tools)
- Customers are informed, in advance, of procedures for reporting incidents with the new service and the direct benefits to them by doing so.
- Service and operational level agreements have been agreed upon by Service Desk management.
- Escalation procedures are in place.
- Customer contact points (e.g. Super-users)
- Required second-line checklists and known-error database
- Service availability schedules
- Support staff skill lists
- Details of related third-party support organizations
- Details of all known bugs and known-errors
- Appropriate third-party contract and contact details
- Involved third parties are aware of all procedures and processes in place.
- Details of third-party support and maintenance contracts

Key Considerations

The purpose of a business is to create a mutually beneficial relationship between itself and those that it serves. When it does that well, it will be around tomorrow to do it some more.
– John Woods

The following are some key considerations to keep in mind, when implementing the Service Desk function. Information collected here is used in many of the other process areas, so it is important to record as much information as may be required to support the activities of those processes.

Service Desk will normally be the first IT group to be aware that SLA targets are in danger of being breached. Therefore, Service Desk requires:

- Information about SLA targets
- Authority to do whatever is necessary to ensure SLA targets are not breached

Escalation procedures and triggers are crucial to maintaining SLA targets. The Service Desk must know exactly how to bring in additional help and exactly what criteria to use to determine when to call in help. There should be clear triggers and thresholds available to Service Desk staff that are reinforced through not only technology, but also process and procedure. The procedure for escalation should be clearly documented and Service Desk staff must be empowered to escalate when appropriate.

As part of their SLA duties, it is important that Service Desk have an accurate and up to date service catalogue that details each service in production and their given levels of service. A service catalogue is a concept that is discussed in more detail in the service level management section. In short, it is a list of every customer facing IT service with the differing levels of service offered for each.

As the primary end-user interface to IT, the Service Desk should always be focused on end-user satisfaction.

It is important that second level support and problem resolution staff maintain an understanding of the service nature of IT. As such, they should be regularly rotated through service with the Service Desk so that they maintain first-hand customer service skills, and so that they can help keep Service Desk procedures accurate and up to date. Placing the staff responsible for developing and maintaining Service Desk procedures into the Service Desk role from time to time, increases the organization's ability to keep procedures up to date and relevant for changing circumstances.

In order to deliver the most efficient service, the Service Desk should have a 'known-error database' that lists all known errors, their status, and an appropriate work around at its disposal. This should be provided and kept up to date by problem, change, release, and configuration management.

Staff Attributes

The quality of our work depends on the quality of our people.
– Anonymous

Service Desk staff is critical to the success of IT, and they need both technical and professional skills to do the job correctly. Service Desk staff should be:

- End-user focused
- Articulate and methodical
- Trained in interpersonal skills
- Multilingual if required
- Able to understand the business's objectives

They should also be able to understand and accept that:

- The end-user's problem affects the business.
- Without the end-user, there is no support department.
- The end-user is an expert in his/her own field.
- They must be genuine in desire to deliver a first class service.

Service Desk staff should be prepared to work in a team driven environment with an end-user focus. They should have the ability to empathize with the end-user and treat the end-user's problem as their own. In short, they should be professionals, who are prepared to support the needs of the business.

Some key things to keep in mind when working with customers:

- First impressions set the stage for all succeeding encounters; ensure that the first impression is a good one.
- End-users calling the Service Desk are typically under stress related to the reported incident. The Service Desk should convey the feeling that it has taken ownership of the incident and is treating the end-user concerns as if it were their own.
- No one enjoys being talked down to or belittled. End-users are experts in their fields and should not be expected to be technical experts. The Service

Desk should, therefore, always use appropriate end-user language and limit the technical speak to an appropriate level for each end-user.

- Remembering that end-users have a responsibility to produce value in their jobs. Technology failures limit end-users ability to produce value and, therefore, create significant levels of stress. The Service Desk should always attempt to evaluate an incident from the end-users point of view and act accordingly.
- One of the primary responsibilities of the Service Desk, as the single point of contact, is to manage end-user perception of IT. Perception is often more important than reality when dealing with people. Therefore, how an incident is handled is often more important than how effectively it was resolved. Service Desk staff should take the time to introduce themselves and ensure the end-user that they will receive prompt, professional, and courteous service.
- Service Desk staff should be well versed in active listening skills and should always allow end-users to express themselves completely, before jumping to conclusions and speaking over the users.

Critical Success Factors

To my customer. I may not have the answer, but I'll find it. I may not have the time, but I'll make it.
– Anonymous

Students should be aware of the critical success factors that ITIL lists for the Service Desk:

- Business needs are understood.
- Customer requirements are understood.
- Investment is made in training for customers, support teams and Service Desk staff.
- Service objectives, goals and deliverables are clearly defined.
- Service levels are practical, agreed upon, and regularly reviewed.
- The benefits are accepted by the business.

Conclusion

We have highlighted that the Service Desk is considered a function in ITIL not a process. It acts as a front-end for many of the other process areas; collecting basic information and often forwarding requests on to other groups. Part of the goal of the Service Desk is to be a single point of contact for end-users. One important reason for this is to ensure that end-user perception is managed effectively. In short the Service Desk in ITIL is designed to simplify as much as possible an end-user experience when interacting with IT and ensures that end-users gain as much value as possible from their technology tools.

Exam Preparation Questions

1. What is the goal of the Service Desk?
2. List five things that the Service Desk requires from Release Management to support new services?
3. Should the Service Desk be the single point of contact with IT for end-users? Why?
4. What are the three types of Service Desk structures?
5. What are the common Service Desk functions?
6. Which requests should be recorded by the Service Desk? Why?
7. What is "follow-the-sun" support?
8. Why should Service Desk set expectations for response times?
9. Why does Service Desk need information about SLA targets?
10. Why does Service Desk need a known error database?
11. What key attributes should Service Desk staff have?
12. What are the critical success factors for the Service Desk?

4

Incident Management

Introduction

Details often kill initiative, but there have been few successful men who weren't good at details. Don't ignore details. Lick them.
– William B. Given

Incident Management is one of five process areas documented in Service Support and the first of eleven process areas covered in this book. The primary concern of this process area is to ensure rapid restoration of service when incidents do occur and to provide information about incidents and incident handling to the other process areas that rely on incident data to perform their activities.

This requires good planning on the part of Incident Management to ensure not only that responses to incidents as they happen are rapid and effective, but also that all information required to support proactive activities in other process areas is collected accurately, timely, and completely.

Goal of Incident Management

The goal of Incident Management is to restore normal service operation as quickly as possible with minimum disruption to the business, thus ensuring that the best achievable levels of availability and service are maintained

Identifying root cause is not a function of Incident Management, nor as already introduced, is it a function of the Service Desk. Identifying root cause of errors in the infrastructure is a costly activity that is measured primarily in terms of unplanned downtime and resource utilization. Restoration of service is generally much less costly in terms of both unplanned downtime and use of resources.

For this reason, ITIL suggests that identifying root cause should only take place when a management decision is made to do so or when a predetermined[1] threshold is reached. Given that the activities involved with root cause identification are at odds with the goal of Incident Management, this activity becomes part of Problem Management.

Incident Management is responsible for looking for incident trends or incidents of significant magnitude that may warrant investment in root cause identification activities. When this occurs, Incident Management presents the evidence to Problem Management, where a decision is made about pursuing root cause identification. During this process, Incident Management should continue working to restore service as rapidly as possible. Only if a decision is made to pursue root cause identification should Incident Management cease restoration of service efforts.

The decision to pursue root cause identification results in the creation of a problem record. The incident remains open and is linked to the new problem record. At no point in the process does incident management abdicate ownership of the incident or does Problem Management take over the incident. Incident Management always retains ownership and responsibility for incidents while Problem Management retains ownership of problems.

---

1. Thresholds are set by management and are equivalent to a predetermined management decision.

Incident Life Cycle

Doing little things well is the way towards doing big things better.
– Anonymous

The lifecycle of an incident begins when the incident is detected and ends when the incident record is closed. During the entire lifecycle, Incident Management through the Service Desk maintains ownership of the incident and responsibility for incident monitoring, incident tracking, and communication of incident status and details to end-users.

Incident Management is the process responsible for managing incidents. Service Desk is often the functional group that handles the incidents and that always has responsibility for being the single point of contact for end-users. All communications to or from end-users should be coordinated through the Service Desk.

The status attribute of an incident record will identify where in the lifecycle an incident is at any given time. This is sometimes termed “workflow position.” Some of the activities in the incident lifecycle are:

- Incident detecting and recording
- Incident classification and support
- Investigation and diagnosis
- Resolution and recovery
- Incident closure
- Service request process

Service Requests, incidents that are not the result of errors in the infrastructure, are normally handled by a process or set of procedures that fall outside the realm of Incident Management. Some requests such as password resets may be handled entirely within the Service Desk, while others, such as more involved requests for change, will be recorded and forwarded to the appropriate support group.

Examples of Service Requests are:

- Request for password reset
- Request for access to restricted data
- Request for information
- Request for training
- Request for change

During the incident life cycle, there are many times when an incident may be escalated to a higher level of support or brought to management's attention. ITIL identifies two types of escalation: "Functional Escalation" and "Hierarchical Escalation."

Functional escalation occurs when greater or different technical expertise is required; for example, when the Service Desk escalates an incident to second or third level support because a greater degree of technical knowledge is required to resolve the incident. Hierarchical escalation occurs when more management attention or a higher level of management attention is required. Some examples are when the end-user is irate, the incident has political implications, or an SLA threshold has been reached.

The Infrastructure Error Chain of Events

Always define your terms.
– Eric Partridge

Every error in the infrastructure has the potential to spawn a chain of events that proceeds from an error in the infrastructure to a structural resolution being implemented. There are many steps along this chain each with its own unique terminology and criteria for instantiation. The infrastructure error chain of events graphic, Figure 4-1, illustrates each link in the chain, its relationship to the previous link, and its relationship to the following link. This chain of events when followed to its conclusion requires communication and cooperation between multiple process areas and the Service Desk. The chain begins with an error in the infrastructure.

An error in the infrastructure causes a disruption in service. This disruption causes an end-user to call the Service Desk where an incident record is created. If service is restored by the Service Desk, the progression usually ends there. Otherwise, in the process of resolving the incident, decision points are reached, such as when the incident is causing too much negative impact to the business. These decision points require Problem Management to make a decision about opening a problem record to investigate root cause or maintaining the effort in the Incident Management process.

The exception is when multiple incidents of the same type, even though easily resolved, indicate that an underlying error needs to be evaluated. In this case a trend report is provided to Problem Management where a problem record may be opened.

There are some important distinctions between incident records and problem records that should be noted:

- Incidents are defined as any event which is not part of the standard operation of a service and which causes or may cause an interruption to or a reduction in the quality of that service.
- A problem is defined as the unknown underlying cause of one or more incidents.
- Incident records are primarily end-user focused. They begin when the end-user contacts the Service Desk and end when service is restored.
- Problem records begin with an IT management decision to invest IT resources and end-user downtime in root cause investigation and end when a structural resolution is implemented.
- Problem records can remain open long after temporary work-arounds have restored end-user service.
- Problem records are focused on internal IT processes and can be the result of a single incident or of many related incidents.
- Management reporting about incidents should focus on measurements and communicate end-user downtime and its impact on the business.
- Management reporting about problems should focus on measurements and communicate IT process performance in identifying root cause and implementing structural resolutions.

Much of the inadequacy of current incident and problem reporting can be traced to the activity of treating incidents and problems as the same types of records with the same basic process for resolution. By separating both the incident and problem records and the incident and problem processes, organizations can begin to produce management reports that provide specific and actionable information. Actionable information is a basic requirement for effective operational improvement.

Incident records and problem records are separate records that serve different purposes. When an incident results in creation of a problem record, links between the incident and the problem should be maintained, thus ensuring that information about the relationships between incidents and problems can be measured and acted upon by management.

Incidents do not become problems and the problem manager never takes over difficult incidents.

What can happen is that an incident causes a problem record to be created, resulting in initiating the Problem Management process. Opening of a problem record ensures that a decision will be made to determine

allocation of resources and investment in downtime for investigating and potentially resolving the root causes of errors in the infrastructure.

At the point where a decision is made to open a problem record, the incident may or may not remain open dependent on whether end-user service has been restored through a work-around. Once Problem Management personnel investigate a problem and identify the root cause, the status of the problem record is changed to "known-error" and a known-error record is created in the known-error database. As with incidents and problems, the problem record and the known-error record associated with it should be linked ensuring that information about the relationships between problems and known-errors can be measured and acted upon by management.

Typically a known-error requires that a work-around be identified allowing the Service Desk to restore service to the end-user while changes to the infrastructure are being implemented. In reality, there will be times when root cause has been identified and no work-around is possible. It will be up to the organization to decide if creating a known-error record has value. ITIL does not address this contingency.

The ITIL definition of known-error seems to indicate that a work-around must exist for a known-error to exist.

The known-error database is a collection of known errors identified in multiple process areas and in the IT development group. It is made available to every process area that may have need of the information. It is particularly valuable to the organization when utilized by the Service Desk to resolve incidents and when utilized by Problem Management to resolve problems.

Once root cause is identified, the next step is deciding whether a change to the infrastructure is warranted. Problem Management initiates a request for change (RFC) that is submitted to Change Management. Change Management determines whether a change will be implemented or if the known-error must simply be tolerated, typically because the cost of change is too high.

If the change is approved, Release Management will normally implement the change. Once the change is implemented and it is verified that the error in the infrastructure is eliminated, the RFC is closed. Closing the RFC results in a cascading close of known-error records, problem records, and any related incident records that remain open.

To recap, the chain begins with an error in the infrastructure that results in an incident. The incident may or may not result in a problem record being opened. Root cause investigation proceeds until the CI at fault is identified. Once the CI is identified and a work-around is identified then a known-error exists. Problem Management creates a request for change (RFC) and submits it to Change Management where it is either approved or rejected. If approved, Release Management will build and implement the change resulting in a structural resolution. That, in turn, causes all open records to be closed.

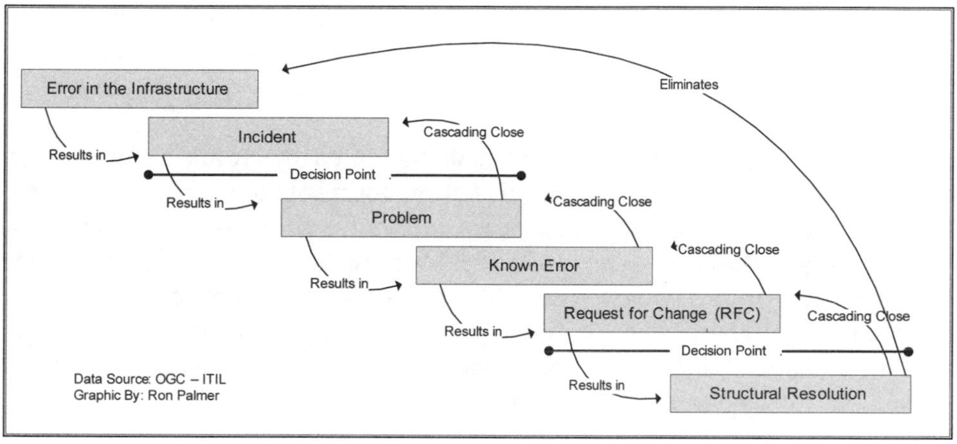

Figure 4-1: Infrastructure error chain of events

Incident Management Process

If you can't describe what you are doing as a process, you don't know what you're doing.
– Dr. W. Edwards Deming

The incident management process diagram shows major flows of the incident management process. Incidents are generated from a number of different sources. End-users open incidents through the service desk. Computer operations staff identify incidents through technical means (monitoring) before they are detected by end-users. Networking staff identify incidents in numerous ways, and IT staff, following normal processes or procedures, identify incidents before they impact end-users.

Incidents enter the process and are either routed to another process as service requests (i.e. RFC goes to Change Management), or are handled as incidents. The Incident Management process has a number of activities that produce inputs and outputs to tools and other processes. Incidents may result in a problem being identified and a problem record being opened. Further, an incident may be related to a known-error resulting in a work-around being pulled from the known-error database.

Resolution of problems and implementation of change result in communication flows into Incident Management that allow for resolution and closure of outstanding incidents. Finally, every access to information, whether retrieving information to be used in resolving incidents or creating and storing information that is collected or created in the process, is a flow out of or into the Configuration Management Database. The Configuration Management Database is a management information system that collects data from all the process areas and makes it available in a usable form to all the other process areas.

One of the inputs to the Incident Management process should be alerts from monitoring activities. An important consideration in ITIL is that any event that is not part of normal service and that may interrupt service is logged as an incident. This means that automatic monitoring tools, which generate alerts, should be generating incidents. Often, system administrators have created highly complex monitoring systems that are not monitored or controlled at the management level. Although well-intentioned, these unmanaged systems expose the organization to unidentified operational risks, such as important trend information that goes unevaluated. Routing these alerts through the Service Desk and the Incident Management process provides several organizational benefits:

- The impact of activities resulting from monitoring can be measured.
- Staff utilization, previously unrecorded, can be recorded and managed resulting in:
    - More accurate cost accounting.
    - Increased allocation for staffing.
    - Reduced cost of staffing.
    - Improved resource utilization.
    - More consistent response by appropriate technical resource.
    - Reduced fatigue.
    - Improving morale.
- Operational risks are identified.

- IT management has access to useful information that potentially impacts goals.
- Proactive problem resolution is improved.

Too often, management has little visibility into the daily exposure to technical risk and the impact on resources allocated to resolving these day-to-day issues. There is often little or no organized effort to evaluate the potential impact of monitoring system alerts; there is little trend analysis being done and the alerts are seldom compared to incidents and problems to identify potential trends. Furthermore, the impacts on IT personnel are seldom fully realized. For example, how often are IT personnel paged after hours, what percentage of those pages could wait until normal working hours, how much after hours time is being logged, what is the impact on productivity and quality from exhausted personnel? These are basic management questions that must be asked and answered to maximize organizational effectiveness and efficiency.

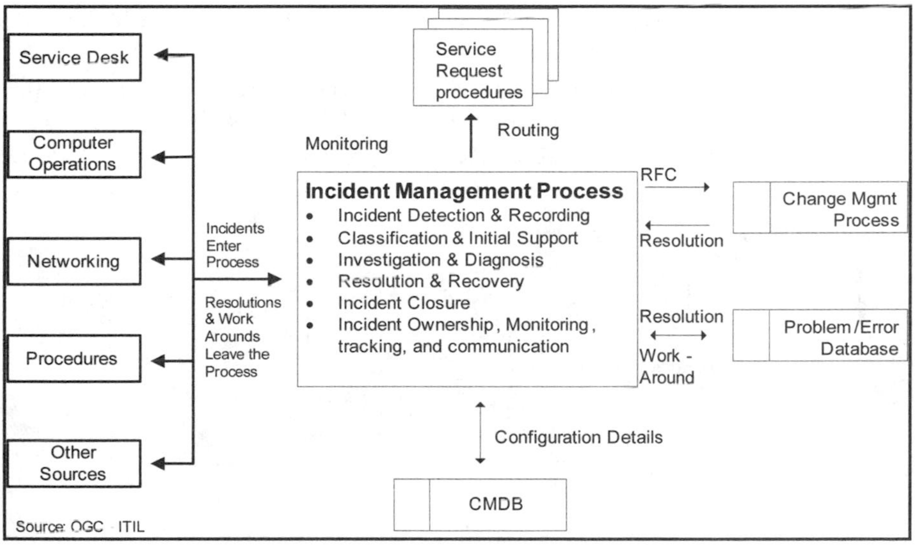

Figure 4-2: Incident Management process

Activities of Incident Management

You can't stand still.

– Proverb

There are six primary activities in the Incident Management process. For each of these activities, ITIL identifies actions and outputs. The six activities are:

1. Incident detection and recording
    - Action:
        - Record basic details of the incident
        - Alert specialist support groups as necessary
        - Start procedures for handling the service request
    - Output:
        - Updated details of incidents
        - The recognition of any errors in the configuration management data base (CMDB)
        - Notice to end-users when an incident has been resolved

2. Classification and initial support
    - Action:
        - Classifying incidents
        - Matching against known-errors and problems
        - Informing Problem Management of potential new problems and of unmatched or multiple similar incidents
        - Assigning impact and urgency; therefore defining priority
        - Assessing related configuration details
        - Providing initial support
        - Closing or routing incident
        - User communication
    - Output:
        - RFC for incident resolution
        - Updated incident details
        - Work-around for incidents
        - Incident routed to upper level support

3. Investigation and diagnosis
    - Action:
        - Assessment of incident details
        - Collection and analysis of all related information
        - Resolution, work-around, or route to upper level support
    - Output:
        - Updated incident details
        - Selection of a work-around

4. Resolution and recovery
    - Action:
        - Resolve the incident or raise RFC
        - Take recovery actions
        - Resolved incident, including recovery details

    - Updated incident details
- Output:
    - RFC for future incident resolution

5. Incident Closure
    - Action:
        - Confirmation of resolution with end-user
        - Set the close category
        - Close incident
    - Output:
        - Updated incident detail
        - Closed incident record

6. Ownership, monitoring, tracking and communication
    - Action:
        - Monitor incidents
        - Escalate incidents
        - End-user communication
    - Output:
        - Management reports on incident progress
        - Escalated incident details
        - Customer reports and communication

Incident Classification

The process of classifying and matching incidents allows Incident Management to be carried out with more speed and minimum use of next level support. Although the Service Desk assigns an initial classification to every incident, as the Incident Management process collects more information, the classification may change. There may also be multiple levels of classification, i.e. a "failure" may be a "software" or "hardware" failure, and further it may be identified by "type," "model," etc.

Classification is used to:

- Specify the affected service.
- Associate with controlling SLA.
- Identify appropriate support group.
- Identify priority.
- Determine checklists or procedures to use.
- Determine reporting requirements.
- Assist in identifying known-errors or solutions.

Appendix B, Table 1, shows an example of a coding system for incident/ request clarification.

Incident Priority

When addressing multiple incidents at once, Incident Management must determine the order in which each incident is resolved and the expected amount of effort required for each incident. This is achieved by setting a priority for each incident, which is determined by:

- The impact on the business.
- The urgency to the business.
- The size, scope, and complexity of the incident.
- The resources available for coping in the meantime, and for correcting the fault.

It may be that an incident with a large impact but a low urgency will have a lower priority than an incident with low impact but high urgency and vice versa. It is the combination of the elements that determines the priority. Effectively balancing these elements has a significant impact on the perception of IT by end-users; as one of the primary concerns of end-users is incident response time.

Sometimes this list is abbreviated and students may see only two choices for a question about what makes up incident priority. Most often, the abbreviation states that priority results from a combination of impact and urgency.

Priority may also be impacted by the effort required to resolve the incident. A low impact, low urgency incident may be given a high priority simply because the resources required to resolve it are minimal. One example would be a service request for a password reset that is given a higher priority than a complicated incident impacting many end-users. Since the password reset can be accomplished within a few minutes at most, it is a good idea to resolve that issue before starting a complicated and lengthy resolution.

Appendix B, Tables 2 and 3, show examples of a priority coding system and the definition of each priority code respectively.

Benefits of Incident Management

The greatest improvement in the productive powers of labor ... seems to have been the effects of the division of labor.
– Adam Smith

Many organizations do not invest in an incident management process that is separate from the activities of their Help Desk. For this reason, it is important to be aware of the many benefits that Incident Management provides. Prepared with this information, IT managers can demonstrate the value of incident management to the appropriate decision makers.

Very often, help desks have grown over time in an effort to benefit end-users. Very few were actually designed and built with a defined structure. This has resulted in help desks that perform some activities very well while performing other activities poorly or not at all. Often the problem is that the Help Desk attempts to do all things for all people—confusing incident resolution with problem resolution and implementing changes themselves—resulting in inconsistent experiences for end-users and an inefficient use of resources.

Clearly defining and implementing Incident Management, including separation of processes and clearly defining goals, bring great organizational benefits such as:

Business benefits:

- Reduced business impact of incidents by timely resolution, thereby increasing effectiveness
- The proactive identification of beneficial system enhancements and amendments
- The availability of business-focused management information related to the SLA

IT benefits:

- Improved monitoring, allowing performance against SLA targets to be accurately measured
- Improved management information on aspects of service quality
- Better staff utilization, leading to greater efficiency
- Elimination of lost or incorrect incidents and service requests
- More accurate CMDB information
- Improved user and customer satisfaction

Critical Success Factors

You've removed most of the roadblocks to success when you've learnt the difference between motion and direction.
– Bill Copeland

Critical success factors must be identified and in place for any process implementation to be effective. ITIL identifies the following critical success factors for Incident Management:

- A working CMDB
- A working knowledge base
- An effective automated system
- Close ties with Service Level Management
- Management ownership

Conclusion

Incident Management is concerned with rapid restoration of service in support of SLAs. Accordingly, it does not pursue root cause analysis. It is also concerned with providing analysis of incident data for use by management and other process areas. Incident Management always maintains ownership, through the Service Desk, of incidents—incidents never turn into problems. Service Requests, such as requests for change, are not considered incidents and are handled through other processes. Incidents may be escalated for many reasons, all of which fall into two categories: functional and hierarchical. Incidents are just one part of the Infrastructure Error Chain of Events.

Incidents come from many sources including automated monitoring tools. Tracking of automated events allows for better use of monitoring data. Incidents should be classified for several reasons including providing the ability to associate incidents with supporting SLAs. Incidents are prioritized based on impact and urgency which provides a method to address them in an appropriate order. Finally, there are many benefits of having a separate incident management process that should be presented to management and evaluated for those organizations that lump all similar activities with the Help Desk.

Exam Preparation Questions

1. What is the goal of Incident Management?
2. At what point does Incident Management relinquish control of an incident?
3. At what point does an incident turn into a problem?
4. How much time should Incident Management spend looking for root causes of incidents?
5. What are the two types of escalation?
6. What are the six activities in Incident Management?
7. Name three things that classification is used for.
8. Priority is determined by which four criteria?
9. List three benefits of implementing Incident Management.
10. What are four of the five critical success factors for Incident Management?
11. Why should alerts from monitoring tools automatically generate incident records?
12. Can incident classifications change? Why?
13. Be able to define the following in ITIL terms:
    1. Incident
    2. Service request
    3. Error in the infrastructure (failure)
    4. Fault
    5. Problem
    6. Known-error
    7. RFC

8. Structural resolution
9. Priority
10. Impact
11. Urgency

5

Problem Management

Introduction

Learning is not compulsory... neither is survival.
– Dr. W. Edwards Deming

Problem Management is the process area that has Incident Management and Service Desk within its purview, because it is primarily concerned with eliminating errors in the infrastructure and depends on meaningful and timely information flows from both Service Desk and Incident Management to accomplish its goal. Problem Management defines escalation procedures and triggers for Incident Management and the Service Desk and ensures that Incident Management and the Service Desk successfully identify trends and indications of underlying errors in the infrastructure. The problem manager role then determines when those incidents result in sufficient business disruption to justify investing resources and unplanned downtime investigating root causes.

The immediate focus of ITIL Problem Management is to improve reactive problem resolution, and free up resources that can be used to improve proactive problem resolution. This in turn frees up more resources to do proactive problem resolution. One of the simple ways to improve reactive problem resolution is to create "multidiscipline rapid reaction" teams that meet to jointly investigate root cause for difficult problems. Multidiscipline teams often resolve problems much faster than the traditional approach of working a problem silo by silo. This time savings, if invested in preventative measures, reduces the demand for reactive problem resolution in the future.

Too many organizations today find it difficult to align to the larger needs of the business, primarily because they are so deeply entrenched in day-to-day reactive problem resolution. Freeing the IT organization from this reactive trap should be the first priority of any Problem Manager who wants to see the IT organization transformed into a strategic asset for the business. Reacting to problems, even if personally rewarding, does not add value to the business. Providing problem-free IT services does add value to the business.

Goal of Problem Management

The goals of Problem Management are to minimize the adverse effect on the business of incidents and problems, caused by errors in the infrastructure, and to proactively prevent the occurrence of incidents, problems, and errors.

Problem Management must first identify errors in the infrastructure that may be indicated by one or more incidents. Trend analysis of incident data is one of the primary methods by which Problem Management identifies errors. Although trend analysis is primarily the responsibility of Incident Management, Problem Management is the consumer of the analysis and will set requirements for the structure and content of analysis.

Following identification of an error in the infrastructure, Problem Management must make a decision about whether investment in downtime and resources is warranted. Minimizing adverse effects may require leaving an error uncorrected if the cure is more painful than the illness. However, when the impact of errors in the infrastructure, as evidenced through incidents, becomes too great, Problem Management should eliminate the root cause of the incidents by correcting the error in the infrastructure through a formal change process.

Whenever possible Problem Management should use all available data to predict where errors in the infrastructure may exist and where they may adversely effect the business. Where these errors can be predicted and corrected with little or no adverse effect on the business, they should be corrected before incidents occur.

Incident Management vs. Problem Management

It is not enough to do your best; you must know what to do, and then do your best.
– Dr. W. Edwards Deming

The critical distinction between Incident Management and Problem Management can be defined by their contradictory goals. Incident Management is concerned with restoring service as quickly as possible and maintaining SLA targets, while Problem Management is concerned with finding root causes and eliminating errors. Root cause investigation often requires extended periods of unplanned downtime, exactly what Incident Management is trying to avoid.

Many organizations have difficulty controlling Incident and Problem Management activities. The underlying cause, typically, is that they have the two processes combined, which results in mixed messages about which goal to pursue at any given time. By separating the processes, expectations become very clear. When practicing Incident Management, restoration of service and maintaining service level targets takes precedence. When practicing Problem Management, root cause analysis and eliminating errors takes precedence. This simple clarity of purpose results in significant organizational efficiencies, improves end-user and customer perception of IT, and contributes positively to staff morale.

There are times when underlying problems cause potentially more unplanned downtime in accumulated incidents than is practical within given service levels. Incident Management will identify this type of problem by conducting trend analysis on its collected incident data. Once this type of situation is identified, a problem record will be opened and problem management staff will work towards resolution.

Problem Management also acts as an escalation point for Service Desk and Incident Management, by providing specialized technical resources. In this capacity, Problem Management resources will be working under the Incident Management goal of quickly restoring service. They will not perform root cause investigation, while working as an escalation resource for an incident.

Although not absolutely necessary, it makes sense that Problem Management take the leading role in ensuring that Service Desk, Incident Management, and Problem Management all work together to ensure that the minimum possible disruption of service to the business occurs over time. Problem Management will never take over responsibility for difficult incidents. If there is cause to invest resources and downtime in discovering and eliminating root cause then Problem Management creates a problem record and resolves the problem. The incident remains open and is managed by Incident Management until service is restored to the end-user.

At no point does Problem Management ever take over a difficult incident from Incident Management nor does an incident ever become a problem. Incidents cause problem records to be opened. The incident record remains open as long as the incident remains unresolved and remains the responsibility of Incident Management and the Service Desk. Problem Management works the problem record.

Problem Management staff determine appropriate action based on the type of record against which they are working. If they are recording their activities in an incident record, they operate under the goal of restoring service. If they are recording their activities in a problem record, they operate under the goal of eliminating errors from the infrastructure.

Incidents and problems are intimately related and should always be linked. This means that you can open any problem record and quickly identify every incident that was created as a result of that problem, or put another way, every incident that lead to the problem record being created. Likewise, it is possible to open any incident and quickly identify the problem that caused it, if a problem record was created.

Every problem should be classified with a category and should have a priority assigned that reflects impact and urgency. Categories are a way to help assign problems to the appropriate staff. Appendix B Table 6.1 shows an example of coding structure for problem/error categories:

Problem Priority

When many problems exist, it is important for Problem Management to determine the order in which problems are to be investigated, and the amount of effort to be applied. This is achieved by setting a priority for each problem. Priority is determined by:

- The impact on the business
- The urgency to the business
- The size, scope and complexity of the problem
- The resources available for coping in the meantime and for correcting the fault

It may be that a problem with a large impact but a low urgency will have a lower priority than a problem with low impact but high urgency and vice versa. It is the combination of the elements that determines the priority.

Priority may also be impacted by the effort required to resolve the problem. A low impact, low urgency problem may be given a high priority simply because the resources required to resolve it are minimal.

Appendix B Tables 6.2 shows an example of a priority coding system and Table 6.3 shows the definitions for various priority codes.

Fire Fighting vs. Fire Prevention

Common sense is the knack of seeing things as they are and doing things as they ought to be done.
– Calvin Ellis Stowe

There are two primary roles inherent in the duties of Problem Management: that of responding to problems (fire fighting) and preventing problems (fire prevention). Every organization is faced with emergencies (fires) that occur without warning and that require rapid response by problem resolution teams. However, many of the emergencies that occur in typical organizations are not truly emergencies in that they could have been prevented. The business is beginning to apply the old adage, "Poor planning on your part does not an emergency on our part make."

Just think what our communities would be like if we accepted excuses from the true fire fighters. We use fire fighters in this example, because there are great similarities between the job of a fire fighter and a problem manager. Both have to respond to emergencies and both have to justify their existence when there are no emergencies that require a response. However, the benefits of fire prevention are so apparent in reducing the loss of human life that no one questions the absolute necessity of investing in fire prevention.

IT Problem Managers face the same type of situation and IT emergencies benefit from the same type of proactive approach. Business is beginning to ask hard questions about why IT spends so many resources reacting to problems when they should be preventing problems. Typically, the statement is "Don't tell me about your problems; tell me what you are doing for me today."

The point is a simple one, firefighters are not successful because they invest in the latest and greatest fire fighting technology and race into burning buildings, they are successful because they save lives through prevention and by ensuring that people know how to react appropriately when fires do occur. If IT managers desire to experience a level of success comparable to the success firefighters have earned then they must begin defining success in similar terms.

IT managers who want to preempt these types of confrontations and experience the same level of success will do well to take a page from the Fire Marshall's handbook and begin following preventative measures. For instance:

- In case of virus, IT might teach turn off your computer, call service desk, press one for virus response team.
- To prevent viruses, IT might teach about the importance of virus and firewall protection for remote access and how to configure them.
- As a general preventative measure, IT can craft and enforce policies that reduce the opportunity for problems and minimize the impact when problems do occur.

This is not to say that firefighters do not react extremely well when the inevitable does happen. They practice their responses continuously and develop teams with specialized skills. They also develop cross-discipline teams that respond in unison when necessary. These are all tactics that IT can adopt to improve their reactive capabilities allowing a shift of resources to preventative measures.

Cross-discipline teams are a great component of any problem manager's arsenal. They provide a unique capability to resolve reactive problems very quickly with a minimum expenditure of resources. This results in reduced downtime for end-users and better resource utilization for IT. The idea is simply to have a team with skilled problem resolution personnel from each technology silo that works together in realtime on complex reactive problems. When the silos work together, communication time and errors are reduced, brainstorming impact is increased, and elimination of potential sources or root cause proceeds quickly. Sometimes the problem results from a technology interaction that falls between the cracks of silos. Having the cross discipline-team working together illuminates those cracks to rapidly identify root cause.

Sub-Processes

I knew I was going to take the wrong train, so I left early.
– Yogi Berra

There are four sub-processes within Problem Management:

1. Problem control
2. Error control
3. Proactive problem management
4. Providing information to the support organization

Problem Control is concerned with handling problems in an efficient and effective manner. The aim of problem control is to identify root cause, the CIs[1] that are at fault, and to provide the Service Desk and Incident Management with information and advice on work-arounds, when available. It includes the three activities:

1. Identification and recording
2. Classification
3. Investigation and diagnosis

Error control is concerned with managing known errors through to resolution. This involves submitting RFCs and working with Change and Release Management through successful implementation of the change, as well as maintaining a known error database. It includes five activities:

1. Error identification and recording
2. Error assessment
3. Recording error resolution (raising RFC)
4. Error closure
5. Monitoring problem and error resolution process

Proactive Problem Management is concerned with identifying and eliminating problems before incidents occur. It includes two activities:

1. Trend analysis
2. Targeting support action

Providing information to the support organization is concerned with providing actionable information to other process areas and to IT management? It includes two activities:

1. Providing management information
2. Cascading information

Major Problem Review is concerned with ensuring that the organization learns from its major problems. It strives to identify those activities the organization performed well and those activities it performed poorly to share lessons learned across the entire organization, to benefit from new knowledge, and, most importantly, to prevent the problem from occurring again.

---

1. CI stands for configuration item and indicates the smallest unit or component in the IT infrastructure that the IT organization tracks and understands. It is defined in detail in the Configuration Management chapter.

Roles

The significant problems we face can not be solved at the same level of thinking we were at when we created them.
– Albert Einstein

Problem Manager

The problem manager has a critical role in the organization. Not only does he/she take the leading role in determining when and how incidents become problems, he/she also works closely with Service Level Managers, Capacity Managers, Availability Managers, Change Managers, and Release Managers to enhance reactive & proactive capabilities.

ITIL lists some specific duties for the problem manager:

- Develop and maintain the problem and error control process and supporting systems.
- Review the efficiency and effectiveness of the problem control process.
- Produce management information for the other process areas.
- Manage problem support staff.
- Allocate resources for the support effort.
- Monitor the effectiveness of error control and make recommendations for improving it.
- Develop and maintain problem and error control systems.
- Review the efficiency and effectiveness of proactive Problem Management activities.

Problem Support

Problem support has both reactive and proactive responsibilities:

Reactive Responsibilities

- Identify problems.
- Investigate problems.
- Raise RFCs.
- Monitor progress on known-errors.
- Advise Incident Management on work-arounds.
- Assist with major incidents.

ProActive Responsibilities

- Identify trends and potential problems.
- Raise RFCs.

- Prevent replication of problems across systems.

Conclusion

ITIL Problem Management is concerned with identifying and eliminating errors in the infrastructure with minimal impact to the business. It works in conjunction with Incident Management to ensure the proper mix between quickly restoring service and eliminating errors. Problem Management and Incident Management have opposing goals that drive different behavior, which is one primary reason for separating the processes. Problem Management shares many of the same characteristics as fire departments. They are both responsible for reacting to emergencies, but are exponentially more effective when they focus primarily on prevention.

Exam Preparation Questions

1. What is the goal of Problem Management?
2. What are the key differences between Incident Management and Problem Management?
3. Explain why problem prevention is preferred over reacting to problems as they occur.
4. What are the four sub-processes in Problem Management?
5. List four responsibilities of the problem manager.
6. Why do many organizations have difficulty controlling Incident and Problem Management activities?
7. At what point does Problem Management take over difficult incidents?
8. When should incident and problem records be linked?
9. How should problems be classified?
10. How are the roles of problem manager and fire chief alike?
11. What are the three activities in problem control?
12. What are the five activities in error control?
13. What are the two activities in proactive Problem Management?
14. What is the purpose of the major problem review?
15. Be able to define the following in ITIL terms:
    1. Problem
    2. Impact
    3. Urgency
    4. Priority

6

Change Management

Introduction

Change is the inexorable law of life.
– Dwight D. Eisenhower

Change Management is the process area concerned with managing changes to the IT environment while minimizing unplanned downtime. It relies on Release Management to effectively implement the changes it approves and relies on Configuration Management to provide information about the environment that improves decision making capabilities.

It is widely argued, and supported in data, that most unplanned downtime is a result of changes to the existing infrastructure. Many organizations implement Change Management because of this assertion. However, accepting this assertion is not a requirement to receive benefit from implementing or improving management of change in your organization. There is a straight forward method for evaluating the effectiveness of managed change. It involves the formation of a management feedback loop by linking key records. This chapter will introduce the final component of information that creates this feedback loop, providing hard data to measure managed change effectiveness.

The real value from implementing ITIL comes from improving the way organizations and processes work together focusing on end-users and supporting business goals. ITIL beginners often focus on the benefits of improving whichever process area has most relevance to them. As students become more proficient in service management concepts, they begin to recognize the greater benefit of structuring processes interactions. At the expert level, students will recognize the value of viewing IT from a systems perspective where processes within the system work efficiently individually and in their interactions to create a more powerful system, able to grow and thrive in an ever changing, ever more demanding environment. Change Management is the linchpin of the IT environment, a focal point for interaction between every process area.

Change Management regulates the pulse of Incident Management, Problem Management, the Service Desk, and Release Management. It depends on Configuration Management to provide information in a form that improves its decision making capability, and it ensures that improvements demanded by the business through Service Delivery processes are effectively and efficiently implemented. It even ensures that development projects will effectively make their way into the production environment. In short, Change Management determines whether the IT system as a whole will be weak and anemic or if the system will be vital and strong.

Change in poorly managed systems often causes problems that continuously sap the strength of the organization; whereas in well-managed systems, change continuously increases vitality and strength through a cycle of limited destruction of the old and ineffective infrastructure replaced with new and vital infrastructure. Just as exercise tears down muscle and bone in small increments and replaces it with more and stronger tissue, so too does effective Change Management build a more stable and business aligned IT infrastructure.

The more successful an organization is in implementing changes, the more likely that the organization can maintain high levels of service. When Change Management is implemented poorly, incidents and problems increase in number, in frequency, and in complexity. Organizations are forced to over spend on Service Desk and Problem Management activities just to stand still. Any organization that finds itself in constant fire fighting mode, that is so busy reacting that it has no time to align with the business, is an organization that is crying out for more effective Change Management.

The primary responsibility of Change Management is ownership of the process for making change decisions as well as ownership of the individual change decisions themselves. ITIL provides for an ownership role over the entire Change

Management process that is different from the role of making decisions about individual changes. The primary responsibilities of Change Management are:

- Assessing changes.
- Authorizing changes.
- Ensuring that implementation takes place as scheduled (coordinating changes.)
- Reviewing changes, post implementation review (PIR.)
- Ensuring that business concerns remain the primary concern.
- Ensuring all records are completed.

Change Management is responsible for managing changes to CI. Therefore, it can be said that components of the IT infrastructure fall under managed change if they are CI in the CMDB.

Release Management works under the direction of Change Management and has the responsibility of implementing authorized changes. However, responsibility for coordinating the change remains with Change Management.

Goal of Change Management

The goal of Change Management is to ensure that standardized methods and procedures are used for efficient and prompt handling of all changes in order to minimize the impact of any related incidents upon service.

This means that Change Management must structure its activities and ensure that repetitive activities, such as common changes, are completed in a consistently repeatable fashion. This structure should ensure that use of resources and disruptions to service are minimized while outputs increase in quality, quantity, and consistency. Standard change model is the term ITIL assigns to this concept.

The standard change model concept can be taken even further so that changes that are not routine in nature, but that have similar characteristics to other non-routine changes, can be treated as a model and can be managed in very similar ways, driving process efficiency and increasing quality and consistency of output. For example, a change model can be defined for non-routine changes that have a given range of impact. This range of impact determines the appropriate management level for the change authority; it determines the need for a change advisory board (CAB), the size and make-up of the CAB, and the management level of each member of the CAB. By standardizing those things that can be standardized for non-routine changes, the efficiency and effectiveness of implementation for non-standard changes as a whole increases.

The change model is tied to change category. In other words, the category of the change will determine which change model should be applied. Therefore, good planning when determining a change category structure is essential. The category structure should also be documented sufficiently to allow low-level staff to assign the appropriate category with high accuracy when creating the change record.

Another important benefit resulting from this structure is that incident and problem resolutions become less complicated. Since resolution teams become familiar with how certain types of changes are implemented, they can more effectively resolve issues resulting in less unplanned downtime. Release Management can more easily schedule implementation and provide feedback to Change Management, thus minimizing impact to the business. Configuration Management can more easily document changes resulting in better decisions. Predictability and consistency of output produce these and other benefits that add up over time to significant competitive advantage.

For an organization to achieve the second part of this goal (i.e. minimizing impact to service), two primary change-related capabilities need to be in place. First, the organization needs a comprehensive and effective Change Management process that ensures that all changes are managed in a systematic and consistent manner. This ensures that there is an overall process that works for all parts of the organization. Second, it needs effective technical change managers (Change Authorities) to drive individual changes to successful implementation within the system. In any large organization one change manager can't coordinate all the changes that need to take place. Organizations will need multiple change authorities with differing levels of authority and differing types of technical expertise to ensure that each change is implemented properly within the controls of the overall system.

The needed Change Management improvements are typically more organizational in nature than they are technical. Organizing processes, procedures, and methods of managing and implementing changes is where much of the benefit arises. Because of this, organizations should consider business organization skills as more important than technical skills in the change manager position. This should be a deciding factor when choosing the change manager. The technical skills come into play with the change authority role where technical knowledge about the systems being changed is crucial.

Change Terms

Change is not made without inconvenience, even from worse to better.
– Richard Hooker

There are many terms common to a managed change environment. ITIL documents some of the most important.

Request for Change (RFC)

An RFC is a standardized document that must be in place for any change to occur. It is numbered, tracked, and archived as a critical business document. An RFC should contain:

- A unique identifying number.
- Identification of the Change Authority.
- Reason for change.
- Effect of not implementing the change.
- CI to be changed along with important attributes, i.e. version.
- Contact information of change requester.
- Date of RFC submittal.
- Priority of change.
- Impact and resource assessment.
- Change advisory board (CAB) recommendations.
- Authorization signature, date, and time.
- Implementation schedule.
- Pointer to release plan.
- Pointer to change builder.
- Pointer to back out plan.
- Actual implementation date and time.
- PIR schedule and actual.
- PIR results.
- Risk assessment and management.
- IT Service Continuity impacts and contingency plans.
- Status, i.e. "logged," "assessed," "rejected," "accepted," "sleeping."

Change Authority

For each change, there is only one person who has authority to approve a specific change within the system; that person is the change authority. This is typically a senior technical person or manager, who has the authority and specific knowledge required to evaluate risk vs. reward and make final decisions for any given change. The category of the change determines the level of authority required for the change authority position. For instance, minor impact changes are often approved by senior technical roles or front line managers, while major changes may require CIO level approval. The change authority will be assigned by the process or by IT management and will be documented in the RFC.

The role of change authority is not used consistently in the texts and may not be used consistently in the exams. The student may see a question such as "Who has authority to approve a change?" The choices provided may include "change manager" and "change advisory board (CAB)" but not "change authority". When presented with a question of this type, "change manager" would be the appropriate choice. If all three choices are provided then "change authority" would be the appropriate choice.

The descriptions of the three roles change manager, change authority, and change advisory board are somewhat imprecise in the ITIL texts and even conflicting at times. This author's interpretation and advice for implementation is that the change manager should own the Change Management process, ensure that the process functions properly, have extensive process and organizational experience, and need not be technical. The change authority should own individual changes, have specific technical knowledge in the affected area, hold either a manager or senior technical role, and be held accountable for success of changes owned. The CAB should only be an advisory body whose recommendations are clearly documented, acting as both an asset to the change authority and a check on his/her decision making power.

Change Advisory Board (CAB)

The change advisory board plays an important role in Change Management. It is a group of key stakeholders that serve to advise and assist the change authority in assessing and prioritizing changes. It is an advisory body only and does not have responsibility for final approval of changes. That responsibility lies with the Change Authority, who consults with the CAB and IT management before making final decisions.

The CAB is made up of experts and stakeholders for any given change. Although there is a core group of CAB members, its extended membership changes to match the needs of each given change. This means that every change could in theory have a unique CAB configuration.

Every change that potentially impacts both customers and end-users should include both customer and end-user representation in the CAB.

Physical CAB meetings tend to have more liabilities than advantages. In physical meetings, input from some individuals is only needed for one change. In this case, these individuals spend a lot of unproductive time in meetings. To resolve this, many organizations limit representation in the CAB, which results in less than desirable input to changes and less than optimal change decisions. ITIL suggests that CAB meetings should be virtual and facilitated by technology. For a virtual CAB meeting, the change authority decides, with the help of a formal process, who will make up the CAB for a given change. The change authority then shares the RFC details with the group either through email or a more formal Change Management system. Each member reviews, according to OLA requirements, the RFC details and provides feedback with specific recommendations. If CAB members feel that more discussion is needed, they can conduct discussions at whatever level is deemed necessary. This often takes the form of a quick phone call between two CAB members or sometimes proceeds to a formal face-to-face meeting of the entire group.

This approach increases the pace and quality of Change Management, while ensuring that each change has the appropriate custom CAB configuration. It also provides for full formal CAB meetings when necessary.

ITIL contradicts itself on the topics of change authority and change advisory board. In one place the CAB seems to have authority to approve changes, in another place the CAB is an advisory board only. I am of the opinion that it is more effective to have individuals (change authority) hold authority for decisions and have groups (CAB) in the capacity of oversight or as a check on power. The basis for this is that when groups are accountable, the accountability is shared between all; therefore, negative issues are less likely to be adequately resolved. ITIL seems to follow this same logic because in every process area, ITIL provides for a single process manager to have authority and responsibility over the process.

The change authority seems to have the responsibility to approve individual changes and the change manager seems to have the responsibility of designing and improving the overall process. This is supported in the text and is the explanation I prefer. However, there are instances in the text where ITIL confuses these roles and seems to contradict itself.

Urgent Change Process

When organizations implement formal Change Management, there is often organizational resistance, and many individuals seek any means to avoid the formal process. One typical way to avoid the formal process is to declare the change urgent. Since few formal Change Management processes have provisions for urgent changes, these changes occur outside of the system, leading to unmanaged and unmeasured changes that result in unplanned downtime. For this reason, ITIL stresses the need to have a well defined urgent change process that is flexible enough and fast enough to be followed in urgent situations, yet formal enough to meet all the needs of an effective Change Management process. This enables the change manager to increase the scope and effectiveness of Change Management and to bring more changes within the control of managed change.

Another reason that leads to abuse of an urgent change system is that users can avoid the detailed change/release testing that most Change Management systems require before implementation. The suggested ITIL process says that even if a change is implemented with minimal or no testing prior to implementation, the change should go through full regression testing after the implementation. Organizations that do this often find problems with urgent changes after they have been installed but before they negatively impact the business.

Those organizations then have an opportunity to resolve the problems before they have negative impact. Another benefit of the urgent change process is that it ensures that every change is logged and tracked so that the organization can measure the impact of the urgent changes it implements. For the typical organization, urgent changes represent an unrecognized and unmanaged cost to the organization in unplanned downtime, utilization of IT resources, and lost business opportunity. The ITIL based organization measures these effects and modifies its behavior accordingly.

Change Advisory Board/ Executive Committee (CAB/EC)

Given the importance placed on the urgent change process in ITIL, it is natural that ITIL would have a means of providing urgent assessment and prioritization of changes. The CAB has an Executive Committee (CAB/EC) that is a subset of core CAB membership. This group can convene very quickly to advise and assist the Change Authority (Change Manager) on urgent changes. This committee ensures that Change Authorities have the benefit of sound advice before approving urgent changes.

Forward Schedule of Change (FSC)

The Forward Schedule of Change (FSC) is the change schedule projected out over a significant amount of time. It lists every planned change, its implementation time and date, and its expected impact. This schedule is continuously published to all potential change stakeholders so that unintended and unforeseen consequences of changes can be more effectively identified and minimized prior to implementation. Every planned change should be made public through the FSC as soon as it is approved. Changes with significant business impact should be scheduled to allow enough time between implementation approval and implementation to ensure that every potential stakeholder has an opportunity to voice concerns prior to implementation.

One measure of CAB effectiveness is the number or ratio of approved changes delayed following publication in the FSC due to concerns expressed by unrepresented stakeholders.

The ITIL texts infer that there are two decision points in the change process. One is the approval to build and test a change; the other is approval to implement the change after testing and implementation plans have been reviewed. These approval steps are not called out by separate terms but only inferred. The FSC should be updated at each approval step. At the build-test approval stage, the FSC would show a target implementation date; and at the implementation approval stage, the FSC should get a specific date and time for implementation.

Projected Service Availability (PSA)

Projected Service Availability documents the planned impact to service levels of every scheduled change and should be published with the FSC. The PSA allows stakeholders to understand the impact of any given change on availability targets with sufficient time to adjust accordingly.

The PSA may result in the business requesting a change be rescheduled or in the business adjusting its working schedule to accommodate the change.

Change Model

A change model is an organized and efficient method for managing repetitive changes. Repetitive changes can be highly structured and documented and their potential impact easily predicted. Defining a change model for each repetitive change allows for a faster approval process and even allows for some changes to be pre-approved.

For example, the installation of a desktop computer for a new hire can be highly standardized. The new hire's role determines the make, model and configuration of the computer needed. As part of the new hire process, HR formally notifies IT of the new hire. An RFC is created against the new hire documentation and is automatically approved. Notification is sent to all relevant managers automatically, while installation techs begin implementing the change. This allows for the swift implementation of a common change while also providing formal tracking and management of the change.

For many, this would be considered an example of a service request and not a change request. Whether it is called a service request or a

change request, the advice and the required activities remain the same.

The reason for separating a service request from a change in ITIL is described in terms of overloading Change Management with routine requests for change such as a password reset. The ITIL text considers a password reset request a service request and not a change request.

For this author the distinction between a service request and a request for change doesn't seem to add value as presented. In an IT Service Management world all requests to IT should be a request for service and a change should simply be one of the services offered by IT. The idea that Change Management might be overwhelmed by trivial changes seems to miss the point. Change models and pre-approved changes are designed to deal with large numbers of change requests and routine change requests. It seems that all changes should be managed, some managed in bulk and others managed individually.

Change Management Activities

There is no way to make people like change. You can only make them feel less threatened by it.
– Frederick Hayes

The Change Management process has many activities. The following list represents some of the most common activities identified by ITIL:

- Logging and filtering
- Allocation of priorities
- Categorization
- CAB meetings
- Approval
- Scheduling
- Impact and resource assessment
- Building, testing and implementation
- Urgent changes
- Urgent change building, testing and implementing
- Change review
- Process review

For testing purposes, it is important to recognize the activities associated with each process area or sub-process within a process area.

Priority & Categorization

We are what we repeatedly do. Excellence, then, is not an act but a habit.
– Aristotle

All good Change Management processes require a method to determine the order in which changes will be implemented and a method to group changes so that appropriate authorization and implementation resources can be assigned. In ITIL, a Priority is assigned to each change that determines the relative order in which changes will be authorized and implemented. A category is assigned relative to the risk of impact to the business and, therefore, determines the level of management authority that the change authority must have.

The ITIL text proposes a different purpose for categories in Change Management than it does in Incident Management and Problem Management. I have not heard of this impacting an exam but it does add to the complexity of ITIL. The text does not go into very much detail about the use of change categories except to give three examples.

ITIL offers examples of change priorities and categories as follows:

Priority:

Immediate – Requires action to be taken without delay. Urgent CAB or CAB/EC meetings may need to be convened. Resources may need to be allocated immediately to build such authorized changes.

High – Severely affects some users, or impacts a large number of users and should be given the highest priority for change building, testing and implementation.

Medium – No severe impact, but rectification cannot be deferred until the next scheduled release or upgrade, and should be allocated medium priority for resources.

Low – Justified and necessary, but can wait until the next scheduled release or upgrade and should be allocated resources accordingly.

Category:

Major – Impact to the business is major and/or a very large amount of build or runtime resources will be required, or impact upon other parts of the organization is likely.

Significant – Impact to the business is significant and/or significant build or runtime resources will be required.

Minor – Impact to the business is minor and few build or runtime resources will be required.

The category identifies the impact of the change on the organization and determines the appropriate level for the change authority. For instance:

- A standard change with minor impact may be authorized by a business process or by a senior technical engineer.
- A non-standard change with significant impact may require the change authority to be an IT manager, whose scope of authority matches the scope of the change and may require management level customer representation in the CAB.
- A non-standard change with major impact might require the CIO to be the change authority and involve executive management participation in the CAB.

Change and Project Management

Schedule disaster, functional misfits, and system bugs all arise because the left hand doesn't know what the right hand is doing.... How, then, shall teams communicate with one another? In as many ways as possible.
– Frederick P. Brooks, Jr.

Many IT organizations have change processes that are specific to different parts of the organization. For instance, development may have its own change process, and each operational technical silo may have a change process of its own. In the past, before systems became so tightly integrated and interdependent, this arrangement was tolerable. The current state of highly integrated and interdependent systems, however, requires a more coordinated approach.

In an integrated interdependent environment, all of IT must work together in a concerted effort to meet the needs of the business. Failure to do so, results in a business perception of IT as immature and ineffective. If IT has a change system that allows groups to act independently and tolerates unplanned downtime due to coordination failures, then that business perception is justified.

ITIL suggests that the Change Management process be implemented across all of IT as a whole. This means that all changes are recorded in a common tracking system. It does not mean that operations should control the code development tracking systems of development. It is permissible for IT groups to control changes that are unique and specific to the group such as code changes during development. What is not recommended is that project milestones or project level changes be masked from other groups.

The system should recognize the specific Change Management needs of individual groups while ensuring that cross-group projects are managed in a holistic, coordinated manner. Any project that crosses group boundaries, either during its development or operational lifecycle, should be managed as an IT level change, visible to all change stakeholders.

The central idea is that development and operations work together to deliver technology based services to the business. Those services only have value if they meet the needs of the business in production. It's not sufficient that development create the most "state of the art" application, the application must integrate into the existing production environment in a way that fulfills the service level requirements of the business.

Change Management Roles

All things change, nothing is extinguished.... There is nothing in the whole world which is permanent. Everything flows onward; all things are brought into being with a changing nature; the ages themselves glide by in constant movement.
– Ovid

Change Management has several defined roles that all work together (and indeed may all be the responsibility of a single person in some organizations) to ensure that appropriate changes are authorized and implemented in a timely manner with minimal negative impact to business operations. These roles are Change Manager, Change Authority, Change Advisory Board Representative, Change Advisory Board Executive Committee Representative, and the Release Manager.

Change Manager

The change manager has overall responsibility for the Change Management process as a whole. The change manager in consultation with management must define the goal of the Change Management process and develop a method of measuring its efficiency and effectiveness. He or she also defines the scope of Change Management and its processes. Some of the duties of the change manager are:

- Ensure that RFCs are received, logged, and given a priority or rejected as appropriate.

- Ensure that the appropriate CAB or CAB/EC is convened to review those RFCs that warrant CAB or CAB/EC review.
- Ensure that CAB recommendations are submitted to the appropriate change authority, and that the change authority either accepts or rejects the RFC as appropriate.
- Ensure that the FSC is updated and published through the Service Desk.
- Ensure that Release Management is engaged as appropriate to build, test, and implement the change in accordance with the FSC.
- Ensure that the change log is accurately maintained.
- Ensure that post implementation reviews (PIRs) are scheduled, that they are conducted, and that lessons learned are incorporated into future activities.
- Ensure that appropriate management reports are created and shared through the appropriate management channels.

Change Authority

The change authority is responsible for individual changes and ensures that changes are handled appropriately through to the PIR. This person is usually a technical expert or technical manager with detailed understanding of the technology to be changed as well as understanding the larger environmental implications the change may have. However, for large scale changes that have wide ranging business impact the change authority role may rest with the CIO. Large organizations may have many change authorities all working within a change system that is organized and directed by a change manager.

Change Advisory Board (CAB) Representative

The CAB consists of representatives from each stakeholder group and includes customer, end-user, and IT representatives. The primary purpose of this group is to provide sound advice to the change authority for any given RFC.

Although not specifically addressed by ITIL, each business group should consider defining customer and end-user roles in each of their sub-groups in order to interface with IT and represent their group on changes that directly affect their group. Groups that have customers and end-users actively involved in IT decision making are more likely to maximize the value received from IT.

Change Advisory Board Executive Committee (CAB/EC) Representative

The Change Advisory Board Executive Committee consists of representatives that are available to the change manager on an on-call basis to advise on urgent changes. These individuals are typically core or frequent CAB members who have experience and responsibility over significant domains. The primary purpose of this group is to provide sound advice on very short notice for RFCs that must be reviewed quickly.

Release Manager

The release manager is responsible for receiving authorized changes, building, testing, and implementing the changes as documented and in the time allotted on the forward schedule of change. The Release Manager or designated representative will have a place in every CAB meeting.

Defining Success

The only thing we can predict with certainty is change.
– Jayne Spain

Much of the value in ITIL comes from the interaction between process areas. It is precisely this type of interaction that provides organizations with a primary measure for the effectiveness of their Change Management process as a whole and for individual changes occurring within the process. This measure is created by tying the Incident Management, Problem Management, and Change Management processes together into a feedback loop. The components of this loop are incident records, problem records, and RFCs (change records).

Changes often introduce new errors into the infrastructure. These errors are identified and recorded in incident records. Incidents that have significant impact lead to problems. Previous sections have stated that incident and problem records should always be linked. The feedback loop is closed (created) by linking incidents and problems to RFCs.

Closing the feedback loop provides organizations with a method for measuring and reporting impact from any given change. If a change introduces a few minor incidents but no problems, then it can be considered to have met the test of causing minimum impact to the production environment. If a change can be linked to many incidents and some low category problems, then it can be considered to have a significant impact on the production environment. If a change can be linked to many incidents and many problems or even one high category problem, then it can be considered to have had a serious impact on the production environment.

By aggregating this information for all changes during a given period, organizations begin to understand the impact that Change Management has on the production environment. For instance if the vast majority of changes result in only a few minor incidents then Change Management can be considered effective by this measure. If, on the other hand, if many changes result in significant numbers of major incidents and problems then Change Management needs improvement.

As always single measures can be misleading. An organization that limits the changes it is willing to implement may score well by this measure, but is not likely to be considered responsive by the business.

This concept can be taken even further by identifying incidents that are linked to changes that were not approved through the Change Management process. Measuring unmanaged change in this way indicates how well the Change Management process has been implemented and adopted. For instance, if the number or category of incidents and problems related to unmanaged change is high, then the Change Management process as a whole may be failing.

Change, Incident, Problem Communications

Despite all of the educational and analytical infrastructure that has been built up around the alleged science of management, it still reduced itself to homework, common sense, and good communication.
– Donn Tatum

Business operates in large part on effective communication flows. IT also operates on effective communication flows. In the IT Service Management chapter, we discussed the difficulties many organizations face as a result of organizing IT around technology silos. One of the most significant difficulties was the breakdown in communications between silos. The concept of services was introduced as a means of providing a common cross silo "customer facing" goal to organize activities. Once a common goal is in place, the next step is to ensure that communication flows appropriately between each group.

ITIL proposes two proven techniques for organizing communication flows in a way that is both productive and stable:

1. Mapping communications to processes.
2. Mapping communications to roles.

Business has been mapping communications to processes for long enough to prove beyond a doubt that process-based communication is effective and stable. ITIL suggests that communication flows between processes be defined and documented. The other recommended basis for organizing communication flows is between roles.

The use of roles is new to many in IT, but the concept it represents (i.e. abstraction) is very common in IT. For programmers, the idea of pointers, (an abstract concept) is a difficult idea to grasp but once grasped is quite powerful. Another abstraction, common to all IT is that of the domain name. Domain names such as "Kedarites.com" allow end-users to easily remember the address to common Internet destinations. However, everyone in IT knows that the address is actually represented by a number called an IP address; in this case "216.173.230.62". Computers translate the people friendly "Kedarites.com" into the digital address "216.173.230.62" and connect to the computer hosting that site. Using abstraction in this way allows people to easily access the wealth of information, services, and entertainment found on the Internet.

Another common use of abstraction in IT, that has revolutionized computing in general and the Internet in particular, is the idea of middleware. Before, middleware programmers who created the interface seen by end-users were required to understand in great detail how to communicate with the computer doing the actual work (the server) because they had to communicate with it directly. This resulted in two very expensive problems for IT and the business. First, modifications to the user interface were difficult, time consuming, and very likely to introduce bugs. Second, modifications to the server were more difficult to implement and often broke user interfaces. Middleware resolved these problems.

What is middleware? It is a set of software instructions that sits in between the server (back-end software) and the interface (front-end software.) This set of instructions simply translates commands in a very precise and consistent manner. It provides two primary benefits. For interface programmers specializing in presenting information to end-users, a simplified set of instructions makes their learning process easier and allows them to access different versions and models of servers[1] using the same set of commands. This creates a significant increase in productivity for both interface programmers and end-users. For server side programmers or system administrators, middle-ware allows them to change the server technology without the end-users ever being negatively affected.

Middleware abstracted the servers from the interface and freed both interface programmers and server programmers to focus on their areas of specialization. This is the very same idea that allows you to use your Internet browser to do real work across the Internet. Your browser, the interface, communicates with middleware that in turn accesses your personal banking data, which is stored on your bank's mainframe computer. Without the middleware, there is no way that millions of Internet browsers would be allowed to access mainframe banking data.

1.The concept of middleware is complex in nature. This example is an oversimplification designed to make a specific point.

So, what does all of this have to do with communications in large IT organizations? Communications in large organizations break in much the same way as communications between computer interfaces and servers. People move from job to job and company to company. When communications are defined directly between people, these moves tend to break critical communications flows. Roles operate very much as middleware in that they abstract the communication flows. Communication can be defined between roles, which remain defined and in place even when people move in and out of those roles. Changes can be made to people within the organization and even to organizational structures without breaking the critical communication flows.

In this scenario, we create roles such as change manager and incident manager. These roles have clearly defined communication flows. For instance, the change manager provides the incident manager information about the change schedule and the status of individual changes, and the incident manager provides the change manager with details of incidents that resulted from changes. These flows remain in place even if the people holding the roles change. In fact, if communication flows are well defined and documented between roles, both roles could change hands at the same time and communication would continue effectively, when the roles are filled by new people.

The introduction of services aligned goals to the needs of customers and now the introduction of roles ensures that communication flows are easily documented and consistent even as the organization changes from day to day.

Conclusion

Change Management is concerned with managing changes to the IT environment while minimizing unplanned downtime. It relies on Release Management to implement approved changes and Configuration Management to improve decision making. Change Management is a linchpin that holds all the process areas together ensuring a reliable advancement of the IT environment. Change Management encompasses all of IT but provides for local control of routine development changes. IT uses concepts such as the change advisory board (CAB) and the CMDB to improve decision making. It also ensures that all changes are managed by providing an urgent change process that meets the competing needs for rapid change approval and managed change for those changes that must be implemented immediately and by providing the ability to identify unauthorized changes. It provides for smooth implementation of changes by publishing the forward schedule of changes and the projected service availability. ITIL Change Management is robust and flexible in how it enables organizations to effectively change and grow their organizations while minimizing the negative impacts of change.

Exam Preparation Questions

1. What is the goal of Change Management?
2. What is the responsibility of the change authority?
3. When does the change advisory board make final approval for a change?
4. List five Change Management activities.
5. How is CAB membership determined?
6. Are CAB meetings physical or virtual? Why?
7. List the six responsibilities of Change Management.
8. Should the Change Management process encompass development as well as operations? Why?
9. How do you know if an individual change or the change process as a whole is successful?
10. How is it determined what is to be controlled by managed change and what is not.
11. What is the cost of poor Change Management?
12. How does Change Management implement changes?
13. Why is an urgent change process so important?
14. When is it permissible not to conduct thorough testing of a change?
15. What is the benefit of performing full regression testing on an urgent change after the change has been implemented?
16. What is the purpose of assigning a priority to a change?
17. What is the purpose of assigning a category to a change?
18. How much of IT should be included within Change Management?
19. List five Change Management roles.

20. List four duties of the change manager.

21. What is the role of the release manager?

22. How can the impact of unmanaged change be measured and reported?

23. Be able to define the following in ITIL terms:

    1. CAB/EC

    2. PSA

    3. FSC

    4. Change model

    5. PIR

7

Release Management

Introduction

Never one thing and seldom one person can make for a success. It takes a number of them merging into one perfect whole.
– Marie Dressler

Release Management is concerned with implementing authorized changes into the production environment with minimum negative impact to production. Release Management works for Change Management to build and implement changes that have been authorized by Change Management. In the ITIL model, where Change Management is a holistic process that includes all changes within IT, Release Management works closely with development through all its stages ensuring that final releases fit seamlessly into the production environment. Release Management also has considerable coordination responsibilities with Configuration Management because Release Management actually implements the changes that Configuration Management records.

Release Management is where the rubber meets the road in IT operations. The skill and professionalism of Release Management has impact far beyond its area of direct control. For instance, skill in managing the business critical calendar determines how much business disruption is encountered during business critical periods. Skill in working with development impacts the percentage of development projects that make it into production on time, on budget, and with positive impact on the business. Release Management's skill in working with Configuration Management has great impact on Configuration Management's ability to keep the CMDB current and accurate. The speed with which Release Management implements security fixes and functional improvements directly impacts risk to the business and business productivity. If Change Management is the lynch-pin of the system then Release Management is the engine that moves the system forward.

Project management is the primary skillset used by Release Management. At a basic level of understanding, operational activities are supposed to be ongoing activities and projects are supposed to have finite start and end points. This is true to a point. The Release Management activities are ongoing for the life of the organization. However, organizations must grow and change or else they die. This leads to a continuous need for release activities. If we look at each individual change or release we see that they each meet the classic definition of a project; a temporary effort to achieve a stated goal that has finite start and end points. Each change or release therefore can clearly be defined as an individual project.

If this is the case, then Release Management is clearly responsible for implementing multiple projects simultaneously and for managing multiple projects, each in varying degrees of completion. Therefore, Release Management can improve its performance by adopting project management guidance that has been proven to be effective.

Goal of Release Management

The goal of Release Management is to take a holistic view of a change to an IT service and ensure that all aspects of a release, both technical and non-technical, are considered together.

Release Management is the hands-on working group for Change Management. It builds changes, packages changes, conducts operational testing, and implements authorized changes into the production environment.

Release Management has a number of key activities:

- Release policy and planning
- Release design, build, and configuration
- Release acceptance
- Rollout planning
- Extensive testing to predefined acceptance criteria
- Sign off of release for implementation
- Communication, preparation, and training

- Audits of hardware and software prior to and following the implementation of change
- Installation of new or upgraded hardware
- Storage of controlled software in both centralized and distributed systems
- Release, distribution, and the installation of software

Release Policy

It is a paradox that the greater the decentralization, the greater the need for both leadership and explicit policies from the top management.
– Bruce Henderson

Given the requirements of Release Management to effectively manage many simultaneous projects at varying levels of completion, it is important to set up a structure that provides for completing these disparate projects in a structured and consistent manner that also maximizes the overall success of project implementation.

ITIL suggests the use of policy to ensure that resources are applied in a consistent and predictable manner and that outputs are likewise predictable and consistent. ITIL makes recommendations for specific concerns that should be addressed in a release policy:

Level of IT Infrastructure controlled – Some organizations will make Release Management responsible only for a certain level of CI, allowing technical resources to implement changes that fall below a given threshold of impact to the environment. Others may make Release Management responsible for all changes to the environment. The scope of responsibility and expectations from each group involved in implementing changes needs to be clearly defined and communicated.

Naming and numbering conventions – To ensure that other process areas such as Incident Management, Problem Management, and Configuration Management can effectively and efficiently carry out their responsibilities, ITIL recommends that Release Management implement a naming and numbering system that uniquely identifies every CI and its state of revision.

Back-out plans creation and testing – No matter how effective Release Management is, there will be times when a planned release simply does not work. In these times, a documented and tested back-out plan will mean the difference between unplanned downtime with its associated loss to the business, and continuing to achieve service level targets.

Guidance on documentation – In today's enterprise environments, proper documentation often allows service level targets to be maintained in otherwise disastrous situations. For instance, documentation specifying the proper sequence for restarting a service can mean the difference between minutes of unplanned downtime and hours of unplanned downtime. Documentation policies ensure that documentation exists, that it can be found, and that it can be effectively used.

Business critical calendar – This is a concept that most IT managers intuitively understand; but that is rarely developed and maintained throughout the organization. Every business function has periods when it is exceptionally important that IT services be available and functioning properly. For instance, the critical periods for accounting are month-end, quarter-end, and year-end. No successful IT manager implements changes to accounting systems during these periods unless accounting management is intimately involved in the change.

In large complex organizations, it is impossible for everyone to know which periods are critical for every business customer. Therefore, methods to collect and publish this information must be devised ensuring that everyone working within Release Management or making changes to production services can choose appropriate times to implement changes.

The IT organization needs a policy for developing, maintaining, and observing the business critical calendar that ensures minimum negative impact to business operations.

Major release plans – Applying project management discipline to Release Management means that releases will be treated as projects, each with its own project plan. These plans are the means by which IT management applies control to individual releases and the release process as a whole. Ensuring that release plans are created to an organizational standard and consistently executed provides another tool with which management can ensure consistent levels of quality.

Expected deliverables – Every release has expected deliverables that go along with it, even if it's nothing more than a prepared statement for the Service Desk to announce a change. Each organization needs to determine what deliverables are required for every category of release and ensure that those deliverables accompany every release.

Definitions – IT staff have a language that is unique to IT. This language changes over time, and often two people will use the same term but associate very different meanings for those terms. (This is one of the most common miscommunications.) We assume that others understand our interpretation of the term. This false assumption leads us to view the world through our own lenses of interpretation. People are self-centered in that way. We rarely think that others view things differently than we do.

The resulting miscommunication is often responsible for missed deadlines, missed service level targets, and increased overall cost of IT. It is incumbent upon management to ensure that each organization has an officially adopted definition for all critical terms and to ensure that the terminology is used consistently.

Role of Release Management in planning and developing applications and technology – Release Management must interact with development at some point in the development lifecycle. Often the interaction is limited to "catching" a new system, as development "metaphorically" throws it over the "wall" that typically separates development and operations. The expected level of interaction between these groups should be defined and enforced by management.

ITIL recommends that operations and Release Management become involved with development from the very earliest stages of any development project. In fact, ITIL recommends that all development projects resulting in changes to the production environment be controlled by a change management process involving operations. The result of which is an increased number of successful releases from the end-user and customer perspective.

Documented Release Management control process – This concerns process and procedural controls that have been created to ensure that the release process works efficiently, effectively, and under the control of IT management. It includes activities, such as:

- Review meetings
- Progress assessments (checkpoints or milestones)
- Escalation
- Impact analysis

Creating and managing the definitive software library (DSL) – The definitive software library is an important part of effective Change and Release Management. It ensures that the organization has definitive copies of every make and version of software in each of the environments: development, test, production, and archive. Setting a standard to which the DSL will be maintained will have direct impact on the effectiveness of both Change and Release Management.

Creating and managing the definitive hardware store (DHS) – This is an area that is set aside to securely store hardware that is used to replace failed hardware in the production environment. This hardware is kept on hand to ensure rapid recovery after a hardware failure. For instance, spare hard drives that can be used to quickly replace a failed drive in a disk array. Policy in this area should be heavily influenced by Availability Management.

Release Planning Procedures

The big things you can see with one eye closed. But keep both eyes wide open for the little things. Little things mark the great dividing line between success and failure.
– Jacob Braude

Release Management impacts every process area in the production environment. In addition, its effectiveness and professionalism contributes significantly to the general perception of the development group. The most finely developed product is considered useless by the business if it cannot be effectively deployed. As such, it is critical that Release Management and development invest time and resources into effective release planning for every change built by the development group.

Release Management is the area in operations that is most dependent on structured project management. Each release is a project of limited duration. It begins with an approved RFC and ends with a post implementation review (PIR). Release Management conducts many projects simultaneously, each with its own schedule and deadlines. ITIL strongly recommends the use of a structured project management framework or methodology to ensure maximum success for individual projects and Release Management as a whole.

PRINCE2 is the project management methodology recognized by ITIL and adopted by the British government. In the United States, the Project Management Institute (PMI) is the primary source of project management guidance. Either is appropriate for use in conjunction with ITIL.

Given that many development groups are adopting structured project management disciplines for their development activities, it would be beneficial for Release Management to adopt similar discipline. The coordination requirements between Release Management and development become much easier if both groups recognize the same project definitions, milestones, documentation, and tools.

Release planning should follow best practice project management guidance and incorporate release specific concerns such as:

- Designing, building and deploying IT systems and services
- Software releases and maintenance of the DSL
- Purchasing, installing, moving, and controlling software and hardware
- Management of supporting tools
- Tracking, review, risk management, and problem escalation

Release Management Concepts

People forget how fast you did a job – but they remember how well you did it.
– Howard Newton

There are a number of concepts that are widely used in Release Management. To ensure that every team within Release Management is working in a similar way toward a common goal it is essential that the common terms have definitions accepted by everyone. These are some of the key concepts discussed by ITIL in relation to Release Management:

Release is a collection of authorized changes to an IT service, which are tested and introduced into the live environment together.

Releases are often divided into the following:

Major software release and hardware upgrade – normally contains large areas of new functionality, some of which may make intervening fixes to problems redundant. A major upgrade or release usually supersedes all preceding minor upgrades, releases, and emergency fixes.

Minor software release and hardware upgrade – normally contains small enhancements and fixes, some of which may have already been issued as emergency fixes. A minor upgrade or release usually supersedes all preceding emergency fixes.

Emergency software and hardware fixes – normally contain the corrections to a small number of known problems.

This division of releases most likely is intended to refer to a classification scheme for Release Management. Unfortunately, the text does not specifically define a classification (category) scheme. This division of

releases should not be confused with release types discussed later in this section.

Release Policy and Planning – due to the project based nature of Release Management and the number of concurrent releases at varying stages of completion, well-defined policies and formal planning are required to successfully manage release activities.

Release Unit – the portion of the IT infrastructure that is normally released together.

Organizations often find efficiencies in controlling the level of detail to which certain groups are authorized to implement changes. One of the most effective implementations of this type of policy is in how military organizations allow certain groups to repair equipment. It has little to do with the skill levels of individuals within groups and everything to do with organizational efficiency and Incident Management on a massive scale.

Groups in the military responsible for repairing or installing certain components have well-defined boundaries around what they are permitted to repair. For instance, vehicle mechanics at the company level in the Army are allowed to replace starter motors on vehicle engines. Repairing the starter motors is often a simple task; but company level mechanics are not allowed to repair at that level, they can only replace it from inventory. The broken starter motors are shipped to another group of mechanics who are at the depot level. There they repair the starter motors on an assembly line basis and return them to inventory. In this case, the starter motor would be the repair or "release unit" at the company level.

Every group in the military responsible for repairing or installing equipment is segmented in a similar manner. Not only does this save significant logistical resources and manpower, it also makes restoration of service in combat environments very rapid. This is an area where military and IT organizations are very similar; the need for rapid restoration of service in mission critical environments.

How might this concept be used in an enterprise IT environment? Let's take an order-entry department as a classic example of a structured situation where every workstation in the group is exactly the same and very simply configured. Order entry personnel, generally, are not allowed to store any data on their local machines or install any non-standard software. Typically, all applications needed are client server based and generic at the workstation level. Now, if a particular component in one of the workstations were to fail, what would be better for the business? Would it be better for a technician to open the workstation and begin troubleshooting while the order entry person is idle; or for the technician to quickly replace the complete workstation with a standby machine, allowing the order entry person to quickly return to work?

If the order entry scenario causes difficulty, what if instead of order entry staff we were talking about traders for a brokerage house who are making realtime trades for millions of dollars? Where does the business gain the most efficiency? Replacing the workstation may even be inefficient at the IT level, but if IT exists only to serve the business, then the larger business efficiencies must be the determining factor.

There are other quality drivers for utilizing release or repair units such as leveling production or leveling demand for repair and release resources. These topics are not elaborated upon here because to do so might cause confusion with some questions that may be on the exam.

Release Identification – Every release regardless of size or type needs to be uniquely identifiable. This means that Release Management needs to define an identification plan (scheme) within the release policy and ensure that it is followed.

Release Types:

Full – A release that tests, distributes, and implements all components of a release unit regardless of whether or not they have changed since the last release of the software

Delta – A release that does not replace all component CI within a release unit, but rather includes only those CI that have changed since the last release of the software, somctimes referred to as a 'partial' release.

Package – A release that includes a set of two or more full releases and is tested and introduced into the live environment as a single release. A classic example is Microsoft Office, which is made up of full releases i.e. Word, Excel, and PowerPoint.

These are the release types mentioned in the previous exam note on release divisions. Be careful not to confuse release types with the release divisions, which can be better described as categories. Remember release types are: full, delta, and package.

DSL – definitive software library - What happens in a typical organization when there is catastrophic damage to a hardware component that requires rebuilding form scratch? In many organizations, the existing production configuration would not be definitively known and the exact version of software that was installed is often unknown and unlocatable. This results in a rebuilt component that differs from the previous production component. Sometimes few or no differences are noticed. However, quite often, critical differences in performance or functionality are found. Sometimes they are found immediately and sometimes they are found long after the repair, resulting in significant impact to the business and difficulty troubleshooting.

The more common scenario is a server room with common hardware and no two servers running the same software configuration. Often desktops will be imaged with different software images by different technicians because definitive policies and definitive software libraries are nonexistent. Although this seems to be a trivial issue, it results in inefficient Problem Management, increased numbers of incidents, and increases in overall costs for IT.

The definitive software store is a dedicated location or group of locations where a definitive copy of every version of software in the production environment is stored. It also stores software versions that have been retired and versions that are in development or testing. It provides the capability to restore previous environments for any number of situations, some of which are as critical and as potentially costly as regulatory compliance issues.

Software that is developed or purchased is placed first into the DSL, only then is it moved into another environment. For instance, software that is created in the development environment does not move directly to the testing environment. It moves first into the DSL where it is logged and registered as a development complete version. The test engineers then retrieve the software from the DSL to begin their testing. Following testing, the software is again placed into the DSL, logged and registered as a testing complete version, and then moved into production.

DHS – definitive hardware store - is a location that has backup hardware components that allow for immediate replacement when critical components fail.

CMDB - configuration management database - is a theme that runs through all the process areas and is defined and owned by Configuration Management. It will be discussed in detail in the Configuration Management chapter.

Build management - is native to software development and impacts quality throughout production.

Operational testing - (distinctly different from development testing) is an area where the typical organization falls short, which contributes to significant amounts of unplanned downtime. ITIL makes a distinction between development testing and operational testing pointing out that the business drivers for each are different and the level of understanding of the production environment differs for each. This means that there should be distinctly different stages of testing before any development effort is implemented into the production environment.

Release Management is responsible for maintaining a production testing environment that closely resembles the production environment. Every software package that is to be implemented into the production environment should be thoroughly tested in this environment by an independent entity within Release Management.

Back-out plans – ensure that services can be restored to normal service levels if a roll-out fails. Back-out plans are often not prepared in many IT organizations and stories abound about failed roll-outs and the many days of round-the-clock work that followed.

Even with the best laid plans, roll-outs often fail due to unforeseen events. Having the capability to quickly restore the production environment often makes the difference between maintaining SLA targets and blowing them completely.

Release Activities

Experience is a hard teacher because she gives the test first, the lesson afterward.
– Vernon Law

Figure 7-1 demonstrates the major activities within Release Management and their position in the lifecycle of a change. It demonstrates that Release Management is active in the development environment; that it clearly has a controlled test environment that is separate from the development environment; and that it performs operational level testing on releases based on the live environment into which it will be deployed.

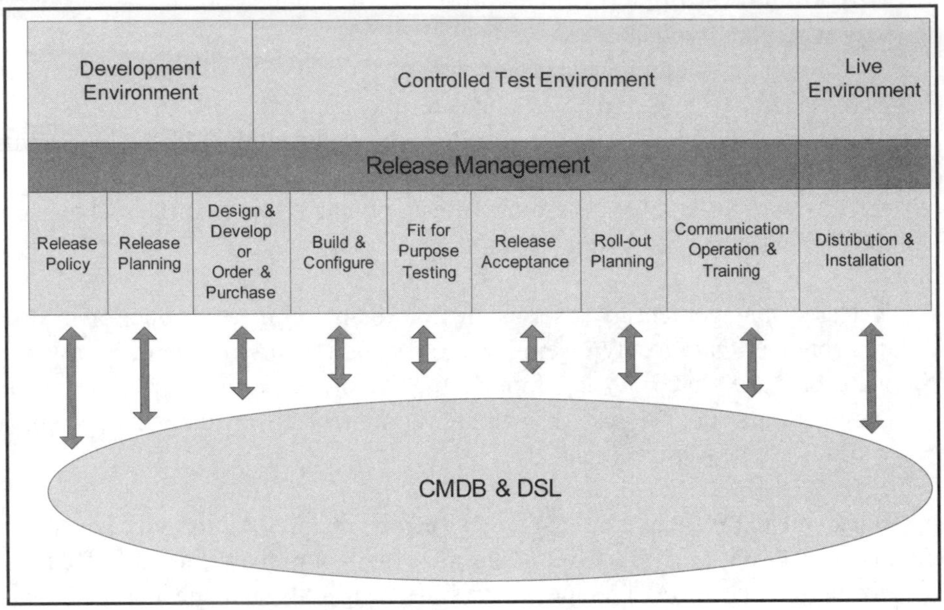

Figure 7-1: Release activities

The major activities and their respective environments are:

- Development Environment:
  - Release policy
  - Release planning
  - Design & develop or order & purchase

  - Controlled test environment
  - Design & develop or order & purchase
  - Build and configure
  - Fit for purpose testing
  - Release acceptance
  - Roll-out planning
  - Communication operation & training

- Live Environment:
  - Distribution & installation

Development and Operations Communication

Nothing is more central to an organization's effectiveness than its ability to transmit accurate, relevant, and understandable information among its members. All the advances of organizations – economy of scale, financial, and technical resources, diverse talents, and contracts, are of no practical value if the organization's members are unaware of what other members require of them and why.
– Saul Gellerman

Many IT organizations suffer from less than optimal communication between development and operations groups. This happens so often that a special term has been created to describe what happens during the transition process. IT people say that developed software is "thrown over the wall" from development to operations. The result is that in-house development projects often fail to meet expectations as conflicts between design and operations are addressed too late in the project lifecycle, if at all. Too many times, this leads to the perception that IT is unable to deliver services in response to business needs.

One way to improve this situation using the concept of services is to create a service for implementing changes to the production environment and to make operations and development jointly responsible for the service. Figure 7-2 represents likely project phases for delivery of such a service with estimates for the level of involvement at each phase based on ITIL guidance.

ITIL describes an environment where operational groups have ongoing relationships with the business at all levels of the organization and where change management is a comprehensive process at the IT organization level. In this scenario, requests for change to the production environment are reviewed and approved by both development and operations, then managed through a common Change Management process.

The process begins with a need being identified by any individual or group authorized to request changes. Because, any change that potentially impacts the production environment must go through formal Change Management, an RFC is initiated through formal channels. The Change Management process determines whether the project should move forward to a build/test phase. This build/test approval kicks off the project management phase.

The change, once build/test approved is sent to Release Management for implementation. If the change requires development then Release Management works with development to formulate a project team that includes both a development contingent and an operations contingent. Early in the project, operations contributes through leveraging its ongoing business relationships to facilitate requirements gathering. Leveraging existing relationships results in time reductions and quality improvements for the functional specifications. Once gathering of requirements is complete, development activities including development testing begins in earnest. Operational activities are minimal at this point, revolving mostly around monitoring the development process for changes that may require a project level change. As the project gets closer to final release, operations activities increase while development activities decrease.

Once development testing is complete, the code is logged into the DSL and the known-error database is updated to reflect all errors identified in development testing. Operations then checks out the code into the production test environment and conducts full operational testing including a pilot implementation if called for in the RFC. The code is then checked into the DSL. Following completion of production testing Release Management submits all the necessary project preparations to Change Management where a final implementation authorization is determined.

During authorization, Release Management and Change Management will determine a schedule for implementation, a schedule for the post implementation review, and publish to the forward schedule of changes. Once Implementation authorization is provided; Release Management, on the scheduled time and date, implements the change into the live environment. Following successful implementation the change initiator is notified that the change has been implemented. From the change initiator's perspective the process is complete. However, from an internal IT perspective there are some vital tasks remaining.

The RFC remains open pending a PIR. Once the time for the PIR is reached, a thorough review of the change is conducted to determine what has gone well and what has not. This feedback is documented and combined with feedback from other reviews. At this point, the RFC can be closed. Once significant feedback has been collected, operations and development will conduct service improvement activities to improve the joint service of creating and implementing changes to the production environment. Successes and failures will be jointly owned by both groups.

This scenario highlights the benefits of following a structured development/project management methodology. Within each methodology, there are clear milestones at each stage of the project. These milestones have formal meetings associated with them, which provide an opportunity for all stakeholders to maintain control over the project and to ensure that the impact of project changes are understood and accounted for by all stakeholders. This provides operations with many opportunities to ensure that the production environment will be prepared to receive the new release on schedule. It also provides development with assurances that operations will accept responsibility for implementing and operating the change in an agreed schedule.

It is critical in modern complex and interrelated IT organizations that development and operations work effectively together. ITIL provides a blueprint for accomplishing this objective.

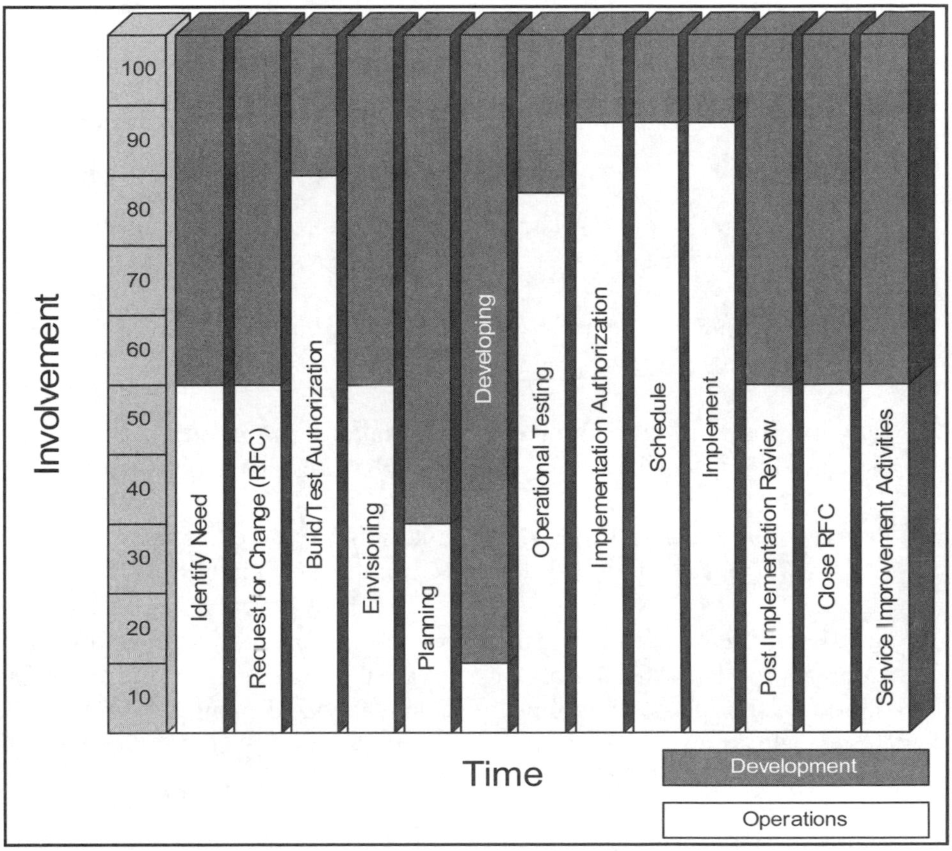

Figure: 7-1:

Key Performance Indicators

Born for success he seemed,
With grace to win, with heart to hold,
With shining gifts that took all eyes.
– Ralf Waldo Emerson

Every process needs to be measured to examine whether it is performing to the expected level. Process performance is measured against key performance Indicators (KPI). The following are some of the important KPI for Release Management:

On schedule & budget – These are standard project management performance indicators that management almost always monitors.

Number of backed out releases – Backed-out releases indicate that more effort needs to go into the planning and testing activities.

Low numbers of build failures – Build failures in production are also an indicator that more effort needs to go into planning and testing activities.

Secure and accurate DSL – The DSL is an important component of a well-managed IT organization and should be continuously maintained.

Legal compliance – Stiff financial penalties accrue for organizations that fail to appropriately license all the software they actually use. There are also significant penalties for failing to account for legal mandates such as the (US) Health Insurance Portability and Accountability Act of 1996 (HIPAA) or Sarbanes-Oxley (SOX).

Accurate distributions – Distributing hardware and software is a process driven activity; therefore, inaccurate distributions are indicators that the process is not achieving the desired goal.

No unauthorized software – Consistency of configuration is a key component in reducing errors in the infrastructure and minimizing the cost of IT.

No wasted licenses – Software licenses are a significant portion of IT expenditures. Keeping the license count at the level required without going over serves to minimize IT costs.

No duplication of effort – If different release groups are performing the same work, it demonstrates a lack of control by Release Management and a waste of IT resources.

Accurate CMDB updates – Release Management is the point where changes are introduced into production and therefore the point where the CMDB sees the most change. Failure to keep the CMDB updated reflects a critical lapse in the process.

Documented PIR for all releases – This indicates that the organization is serious about learning from successes and failures.

Appropriate staffing – There is a level of staffing that is appropriate for meeting the quality levels and schedules required by the business. Significant deviation from that level indicates poor process performance.

Conclusion

Release Management is concerned with implementing only approved changes into the production environment with minimal negative impact to the business. It accomplishes this by applying proven project management methodologies, structured policies to drive consistency, and bestpractices in communications, and working with other IT groups. Release Management works for Change Management in that it only implements approved changes, it interfaces closely with Configuration Management to update records as changes are implemented, and it interfaces with development; ensuring that development benefits from operations maintained relationships with the business and that development projects are effectively released into the live environment in support of business goals.

Exam Preparation Questions

1. What is the goal of Release Management?
2. List the nine Release Management activities.
3. Identify the environment in which each activity operates.
4. Why is policy so important for Release Management?
5. List the 12 specific policy recommendations, provided by ITIL.
6. What is the role of Release Management in planning and developing applications and technology?
7. List the three release types.
8. What is the purpose of a back-out plan? When is it needed?
9. Why might operations need testing that is separate from development testing?
10. List the three environments over which Release Management has responsibility?
11. At what point should Release Management be involved in development of new services?
12. At what point does the development group cease involvement in development of new services?
13. Give an explanation for why all releases might need a unique identification number.
14. What is the purpose of an identification scheme?
15. At what point does development and operations begin communications about a new development project that will result in a change to the production environment?
16. How can operations benefit development in the requirements gathering phase?

17. Which process is responsible for conducting the PIR?

18. Which process areas are involved in the PIR?

19. List five key performance indicators for Release Management.

20. Be able to define the following in ITIL terms:

    1. Release
    2. Release unit
    3. Roll-out
    4. Full release
    5. Delta release
    6. Package release
    7. DSL
    8. DHL
    9. Business critical calendar
    10. PRINCE2

8

Configuration Management

Introduction

To be conscious that you are ignorant of the facts is a great step to knowledge.
– Benjamin Disraeli

IT organizations and systems are growing increasingly complex and integrated. The impact to the business when these systems fail is dramatic. In the past, the heroic actions of a few technical gurus allowed many organizations to maintain an acceptable level of service. Increasingly however, this type of management is failing to produce acceptable levels of service. Furthermore, as recent legislation requires senior executives to personally certify risks to businesses sustainability (US, Sarbanes-Oxley), the risks inherent in this type of management will become increasingly unacceptable.

The only way for organizations of any significant size to provide assurances that their activities are executed within the control parameters provided by corporate and IT governance is to organize those activities within processes. Process tools such as controls, key performance indicators, critical success factors, key goal indicators, and feedback loops provide reliable information that assures activities are operating within acceptable governance parameters.

Governance controls however are primarily implemented to limit the downside risks. IT service management and ITIL not only provide a well accepted structure for implementing governance controls, they also provide the structure and guidance for improving the competitive capabilities of any size or type of organization. The same process tools that ensure compliance also provide the capability to adjust to market demands by increasing production, increasing quality, reducing cost, increasing efficiency, or creating new opportunities to exploit.

To effectively implement governance controls and adjust to market demands, organizations must have accurate, timely, and meaningful information with which to make decisions and to demonstrate compliance. Without information of this type, Change Management becomes only as effective as the change authority's gambling ability. How many investors want to risk their investments on the guess work of the change authority of the day?

Accurate, timely, and meaningful information provides the basis for a consistent improvement in decision making in every process area. As statistics and compound interest have demonstrated for hundreds of years, small improvements in critical areas can have profound implications over time. Would management worry if the company's primary competitor was improving its decision making accuracy by 3% per year, every year, while its own decision making accuracy remained the same? Should it worry?

Today's enterprise environments are complex and interdependent. Often changes that once had little impact now have far reaching impacts that directly affect the business. This complexity has overwhelmed the ability of even the best change authorities to make decisions about changes that minimize negative impact on the business. IT has become very successful at providing information that empowers business decision makers to make better decisions. Ironically, it has done very little to improve the way it makes decisions about IT, even as IT complexity has grown exponentially. One of the roles of Configuration Management is to provide information that improves decision making across all of the process areas.

Configuration Management does this by assembling and presenting information about the IT environment in the form of a configuration management database (CMDB). In each of the previous chapters the terms configuration item (CI) and CMDB have been used with very little explanation of what they are. Now that students have an appreciation for their impact, these topics will be documented in detail.

Goal of Configuration Management

The goal of Configuration Management is to provide a logical model of the IT infrastructure by identifying, controlling, maintaining, and verifying the versions of all configuration items in existence.

Configuration Management seeks to provide the underlying information that IT uses to improve decision making and to effectively visualize, model, and manage modern interdependent IT systems.

Activities

It is a capital mistake to theorize before one has data. Insensibly one begins to twist facts to suit theories instead of theories to suit facts.
– Sir Arthus Conan Doyle

Some of the important activities that occur in this process area are:

- Planning.
- Identification.
- Control.
- Status accounting.
- Verification & audit.

Planning – Planning for Configuration Management includes defining the purpose, scope, objectives, policies, and procedures that facilitate Configuration Management.

Identification – Involves determining the structures by which CI will be organized: defining attributes such as owner, version, status, etc.; defining the interrelationships between CI and CI structures; and entering all information into the CMDB. This activity seems easy on the surface, but becomes exponentially complex in practice. Implementing this activity will take many sequential projects; each designed to take the scope of implementation one step further. Attempting to scope projects that incorporate too many levels of structure is a common cause of failure in the identification activity.

Some organizations begin with an asset register and then add IT focused attributes and relationships between CI. This is an example of starting at a granular level. Other organizations begin at the highest level, defining customer facing services, and then drill down into sub-services and components of those services.

Perhaps the quickest way to implement is to have two groups—one starting with the asset register and the other starting with services—work towards the middle from each end. Each group conducts sequential projects that incrementally increase the scope of CI identification towards a common goal; identification of all CI in the environment.

Control – involves ensuring that CI go through an approved change management process before changes are entered into the CMDB, and that appropriate documentation accompanies the CI in the CMDB. Controlling the information and knowing when the environment has changed requires policies, planning, skilled implementation of process, and applied discipline from management.

Status Accounting – ensures that every status change a CI goes through is recorded so that a history of status changes can be documented. This includes the detailed snapshot information for the CI before and after each status change.

Verification and Audit – ensures that information in the CMDB is accurate over time. It involves conducting reviews and audits to ensure that physical characteristics of CI match what is recorded in the CMDB. (When discrepancies occur, it typically indicates a breakdown in the policies or processes in place to ensure that configuration information is collected and utilized.)

Many, of the activities in Configuration Management are organizational in nature. Perhaps, one of the most important problems organizations face when trying to implement Configuration Management is assigning technical people to fill roles that are primarily organizational in nature and require skills similar to that of a librarian.

Too many people see Configuration Management as an exercise in building a physical database to fill the role of CMDB as described in ITIL. The CMDB is not a physical database. It is better described as a "management information system" or a "decision support system." It brings many data sources together in ways that serve to improve decision making such as the capability to visualize and model complex systems.

The supporting organizational work that is required to achieve the goal of improving decision making is simply not technical in nature. It is organizational, it is managerial, and it requires organizing and structuring data in a way that makes it efficient to retrieve that information when and how it is needed. In many ways it is like building a library.

A library is a decision support system. It collects information from many different data stores: books, periodicals, newspapers, digital archives, etc. Most importantly it provides a system by which informa-

tion can be indexed, stored, and retrieved efficiently and effectively to support decision making. Before anyone would consider collecting thousands of books and periodicals and calling this collection a useful library, they would first find an indexing system that transforms the collection into something useful for decision making.

For hundreds of years libraries did this effectively without computers or electronic technology. The information, indexed by a system such as the Dewey Decimal System, could be easily and effectively accessed by the card catalog file and indexed lists in print form. IT needs a Dewey Decimal system for Configuration Management before spending endless cycles building a database.

Once a system is devised to logically index, store, and retrieve the many disparate bits of data scattered throughout the IT environment then it will be time for IT to employ technical resources to construct databases in support of this logical system.

Configuration Item (CI)

Information is a source of learning. But unless it is organized, processed, and available to the right people in a format for decision making, it is a burden, not a benefit.
– William Pollard

The items an organization tracks and the level of detail maintained significantly impacts an organization's ability to be successful with IT service management. In ITIL, each item of the IT environment that is registered and tracked is called a configuration item or CI. There are many details of CI that also need to be understood. These details are considered attributes of the CI. Attributes can be details; such as, the amount and configuration of memory in a workstation, the number of ports for a switch, the status of a CI, or the unique identifier for that CI. A CI can be anything from a hardware component, to a software component, or a policy, process, accommodation, or even a human resource.

There are many instances where people can be considered CI. For example, Capacity Management needs to understand the number of people available to fill a given role at any given time and the average utilization of those people. Each server in an environment should have an associated escalation list of people who are responsible for that server.

In Change Management, we learned that all configuration items are subject to Change Management. In Configuration Management, we have a definition of a CI as "any item in the IT environment that is subject to managed change." This circular reasoning leads one to wonder which comes first. Does Change Management determine which items become CIs or does Configuration Management determine which items are subject to managed change?

The reality is that determining which items are to be recorded as CI and thus which items are to be under managed change is a management responsibility. Management must decide which items are important enough to the functioning of the IT environment that they should be recorded and tracked throughout their lifecycle. There is benefit to tracking and understanding every item in the IT environment, and there are of course costs associated with doing so. Management determines the level of granularity to which CI are tracked according to the benefits of understanding versus the cost of maintaining the information.

A common decision is whether to track keyboards individually. There may be benefit in tracking each individual keyboard in the environment; however, the costs of keeping that information up to date typically far outweigh the benefits. Most organizations would not track keyboards individually.

However, there may be more benefit in knowing the types of keyboards in the environment by model or other unique usage, i.e. ergonomic. By having a keyboard model as a CI and tracking the CI of keyboard as an attribute for workstations and servers, management can begin to understand the operational costs of one model over another by replacement rate or the repetitive injury rate per model. This information might translate into making a decision to replace all keyboards of one model with another model to reduce the impact of repetitive stress injuries on the business or to reduce support costs related to poor quality. An example of this is when one model of keyboard has a defect rate of twice the average default rate; it probably makes sense to replace all keyboards of that model in one effort thereby eliminating a high number of one-off incidents related to keyboard quality.

Access to information provides significant opportunities for creating value if management understands how to mine the information, and if the organization is agile enough operationally to realize the benefits. The benefits can only be realized if the information exists and is accurate. However, simply having the information is not sufficient; management must invest resources into learning to leverage the information. This is a clear example of where a process-driven organization can begin creating competitive advantage that nonprocess-driven organizations cannot duplicate.

Once management determines which items are to be tracked as CI, the detail information to be tracked for each CI class must be decided. The information needed by each organization is likely to vary considerably. However, there are certain details that ITIL recommends be recorded for every CI:

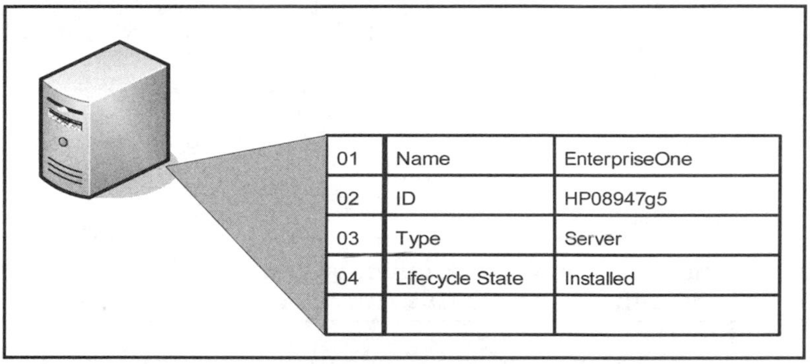

Figure 8-1: Server with attributes

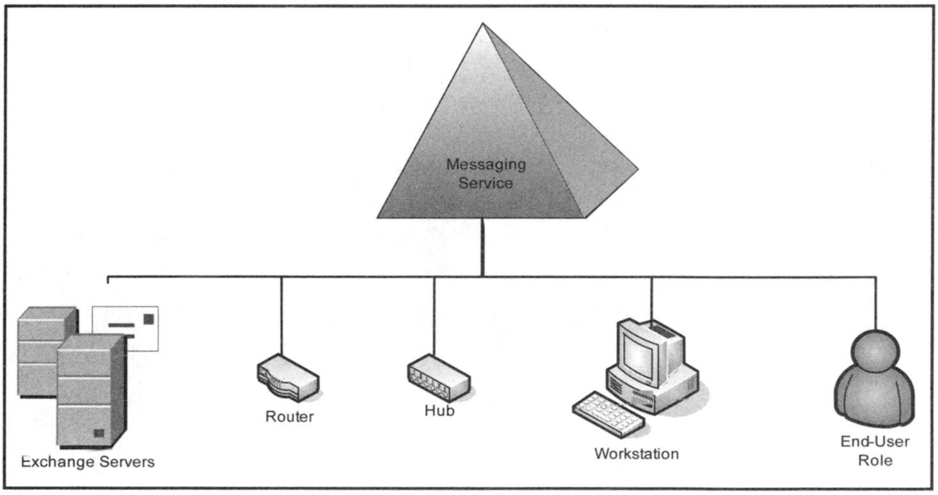

Figure 8-2: Messaging service with components

- Each CI should have a unique identifier that distinguishes it from all other CI.
- CI should be classified into types such as software products, business systems, system software, servers, mainframes, workstations, laptops, routers, hubs, etc.
- CI have 'life cycle states.' For instance, a package application release may be 'registered,' 'accepted,' 'installed,' or 'withdrawn.'

- CI always have relationships to other CI. Figure 8-2 shows a simple service; and the CI that are combined to supply that service. A few examples of how CI can be related are:
    - A CI can be part of another CI; a server is part of a service.
    - A CI can be connected to another CI; a server is connected to a network switch that is connected to a router that is connected to a T1 line.
    - A CI can use another CI; a web server uses (accesses) a database server to present information.

Associating and maintaining relationships (links) between CI is the primary difference between the CMDB and an asset register.

The details associated with each CI are stored and organized as attributes, which represent a common concept in database design. Every field in a database has attributes that describe it. For instance, each field has an attribute that determines what type of data it contains: text, integer, floating point, blob, etc. This is detailed information that does not warrant being categorized as a CI by itself. A classic example is Random Access Memory (RAM). RAM is very important to track, but is typically only useful in reference to the server or workstation in which it is installed. Therefore, it is more efficiently tracked as an attribute not a CI.

There are two attributes that ITIL considers necessary for every CI:

1. Status
2. Unique identifier

Other attributes that CI may have are:

- Revision number
- Manufacturer
- Manufacturer part number
- Manufacturer serial number
- Asset number
- Cost of CI
- Location
- Owner
- Release date
- Planned expiration date
- Configuration information such as:
    - RAM
    - Storage capacity
    - Network connection speed
    - License type

    - Number of licenses
    - Processor type
- ID of service it supports
- Link to documentation

ITIL introduces the concept of variant applied to CI. A variant is a CI that deviates from other similar CI in a significant enough manner that it needs to be tracked separately, but it is still similar enough to the source CI class that it needs to be included in information presented about that CI class. For example, an organization may have 20 servers of "model X." Eighteen of those servers are configured exactly the same, but two are configured significantly differently to warrant tracking them as a class of CI; yet they also remain part of the class model X. These two servers would be tracked as variants of model X so that they can be accounted for as both belonging to the group model X and the group "variant A model X."

Variants are a complex concept and use of variants would typically indicate an organization has a very mature Configuration Management implementation.

Configuration Management Database (CMDB)

Facts apart from their relationships are like labels on empty bottles.
– Sve Halla

The Configuration Management database (CMDB) has been mentioned in almost every chapter to this point. It is the central source of information for all management decisions in IT service management. That makes it an enormous collection of information of many different types and uses. So far, the concepts of an incident database, a problem database, a known-error database, an RFC database, and information required to link incidents, problems, and change records have all been discussed. This data is likely all stored in different physical databases. However, it is all part of the CMDB. This means that the CMDB, in any sizable organization, is not a single database but a collection of many different data stores. It is a virtual concept made up of many physical databases and physical stores of information. It becomes a CMDB when the information is brought together with a common interface that makes the information accessible and relevant for decision makers; most importantly, it becomes a CMDB when the CIs are related (linked) to one another.

Too many organizations take a technical view of the CMDB and begin by trying to develop a database schema in an effort to build a "CMDB." It is important to emphasize again, that the CMDB is not one physical database. It is a logical concept for organizing information, whose closest tangible representation may be a common interface with many collections of information. It is made up of many physical databases, at least one of which will contain the relationships or links between CIs. See Figure 8-3 for a graphical depiction of a simple CMDB with its various data stores, including a data store specifically for keeping links or relationships between CI.

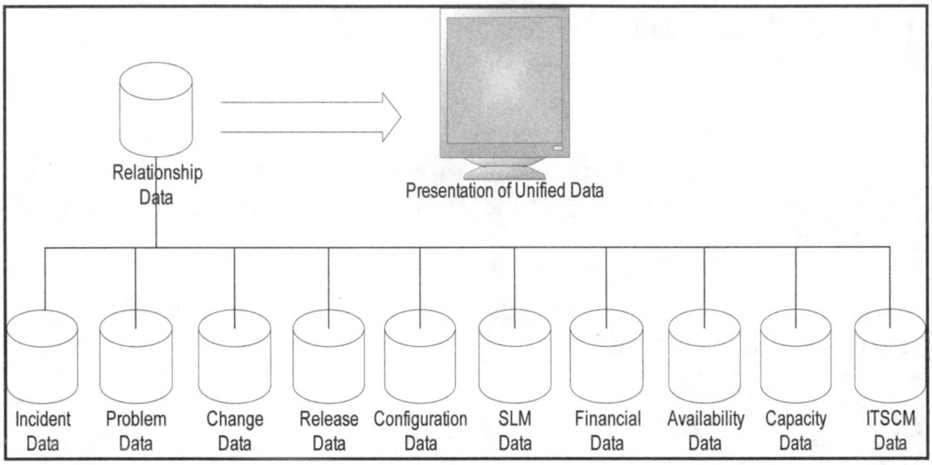

Figure 8-3: Simple CMDB with the data stores introduced by ITIL

One thing that makes a CMDB unique from most data stores is that it focuses on relationships between CIs. That is, it allows decision makers to draw visuals of systems and their interconnections so that they can model the potential impacts of a change to any component or collection of components. Modeling is a powerful tool for understanding and managing complex disciplines.

Every discipline that is required to understand the workings of complex systems ends up building models of those systems, which serve to increase basic understanding and to predict outcomes of changes to the system. As IT environments continue to grow in size and complexity, successful managers will be those who are able to model their environments and accurately predict the effects of change. Scientists build models of many types; physical models that show basic mechanics, mathematical models that incorporate natural laws calculating complex relationships, and visual dynamic models based on the mathematical models that allow for testing concepts and theories. The current state of science would be impossible without models.

Closer to home is the use of models in the finance and accounting field with a tool every IT person is familiar with, spreadsheets. What is arguably the most value contribution from spreadsheets? It is the ability for individuals to build complex financial models and perform what-if scenarios in realtime with real data. Much of what we take for granted in finance today would be impossible without the ability to model.

Home ownership is at all time highs because financial experts are able to build risk models that tell them how to bundle mortgages into marketable assets with highly predictable levels of risk. This allows bundles of mortgages to be sold in the equities markets, increasing the money available in the system for home mortgages and also allowing those with less than stellar credit to get mortgages because their high risk loans are bundled with very low risk loans. Without financial models of this type, our economy would be very different and many things we take for granted in finance today simply would not exist.

IT has made the use of models in all these fields possible. Without information systems and tools like spreadsheets and statistical programs, these disciplines would be limited to very simple models and our knowledge and capabilities would be greatly diminished. The ironic aspect is that IT may actually be one of the last disciplines to utilize the enormous leveraging power of models. We provide the tools but fail to leverage them ourselves, partly because we have not developed the discipline necessary to collect useful information to feed into the models. Configuration Management exists in part to ensure that accurate up-to-date data exists to be used in modeling the IT environment.

Conclusion

Configuration Management provides a process for collecting and presenting information that can be used by the other process areas to improve their own decision making as well as the efficiency and effectiveness of their process activities. It requires an investment in time and resources, primarily nontechnical resources, to implement correctly. However, the result is improvement in efficiency and effectiveness across all of IT including IT governance that not only supports compliance but that leads to increased competitive advantage.

Exam Preparation Questions

1. What is the goal of Configuration Management?
2. List the five Configuration Management activities.
3. List five typical configuration items and describe why they would be considered configuration items.
4. Describe how people could be considered a configuration item.
5. What is the primary difference between the Configuration Management database and an asset register?
6. Is the Configuration Management database a physical database? Explain.
7. What two details should be recorded for every configuration item?
8. Be able to define the following in ITIL terms:
    1. CMDB
    2. CI
    3. Attribute
    4. Status Accounting
    5. Variant

Part III

SERVICE DELIVERY

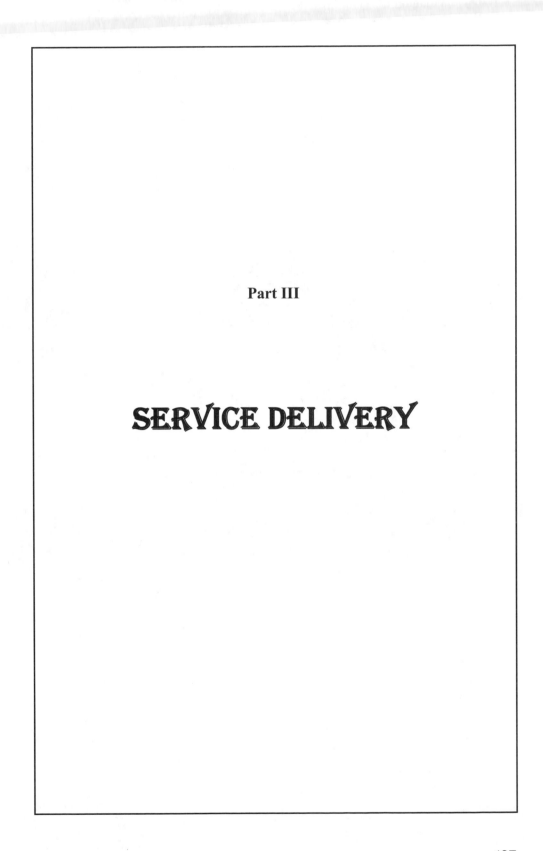

4632596584

Introduction

Part III covers the ITIL book Best Practice for Service Delivery, or the "red book." It is a collection of the five tactical processes:

1. Service Level Management
2. Financial Management for IT Services
3. Capacity Management
4. Availability Management
5. IT Service Continuity Management

These processes are considered tactical in nature because their inputs come from operational processes, they deal primarily with customers, and they begin the transformation of IT centric activities into business aligned activities. These are often considered the interesting processes or the processes that many practitioners of ITIL want to move to immediately. Skipping the operational processes in part II, however, is a rookie mistake.

Once the operational processes are mastered, the tactical processes can begin the transformation process that brings significantly improved business aligned IT services. Those who move into the tactical processes based on solid operational skills can take the game to a higher level. At this level, the game becomes more about transformation of the way IT has traditionally done business. Service level agreements move beyond being just a hope and a prayer. They become relationship building documents that formally recognize the accomplishments of IT. High availability moves from being a heroic feat to an every-day occurrence. Capacity improvements move from being a last minute scramble to the result of a well executed plan. IT ultimately begins to move away from being an expensive "cost of doing business" transforming itself into a valued partner in the eyes of the business.

9

Service Level Management

Introduction

Alignment is mostly about trust, credibility and respect. Only IT leaders who inspire those kinds of feelings in the business leaders ever achieve alignment – and keep it.
– Barbara Gomolski

Service Level Management is the process area directly responsible for managing customer perceptions and relationships. It is responsible for negotiating with customers over the services that are provided by IT, the levels at which those services are delivered, and the prices that are paid for those services. Service Level Management utilizes a tool called a service catalog that serves several purposes in IT service management. It consists in its simplest form as a collection of end-user facing services, standard service levels for each service, and associated costs. Service level agreements (SLAs) define levels of service agreed upon between IT and the business. They are in turn supported by agreements among IT groups, operational level agreements (OLAs), and by contracts with outside vendors (i.e. underpinning contracts (UCs)).

Effective Service Level Management from an ITIL perspective results in healthy working relationships between IT and the business. Only when IT and the business enjoy a healthy working relationship can IT truly align itself with business needs. Service level agreements serve to document existing relationships and the achievement of defined targets. They are not documents of force that require one side or the other to do something they are incapable of or unwilling to do. In other words, they are agreements between business partners working toward the same primary goal.

This is a different concept from what many organizations currently follow. These organizations often attempt to use SLAs to force one party to do something that they could not get them to do any other way. In other words, SLAs are improperly used as band aids for dysfunctional relationships. The results are predictably unsatisfactory because SLAs appear to be coercive rather than cooperative; therefore, this current system provides little or no business confidence that service levels can be guaranteed.

ITIL guidance helps IT organizations learn to build solid relationships with the business. Solid relationships are the foundation of business/IT partnerships that provide lasting benefits to the business in terms of improved responsiveness and closer attention to important business details. In short, the relationship allows IT to understand what is important to the business and to obtain the resources required to deliver what the business needs.

In relationships, communication is a prime indication of wellness. In other words, if you expect to have well-functioning relationships, you must communicate effectively. The same holds true for business. If business intends to succeed (i.e. make money), it must communicate effectively with its customers and within its own organization. As IT strives to align with business goals and to contribute to the success of the business, it must focus on improving and maintaining relationships with customers and end-users by embracing a communication strategy that identifies the needs of each respective party.

– Christine Belaire, Ph.D.

Goal of Service Level Management

The goal of Service Level Management is to maintain and improve IT service quality, through a constant cycle of agreeing, monitoring and reporting upon IT service achievements and instigation of actions to eradicate poor service – in line with business or cost justification.

In ITIL, Service Level Management is concerned with building long-term relationships with the business, which demonstrates the IT department's desire and capability to be a strategic partner with the business. It accomplishes these goals in a number of ways by:

- Helping the business understand and define its service level requirements for the services IT offers
- Demonstrating that IT can deliver the levels of service required and then formalizing service level agreements that document that fact
- Helping the business understand how IT adds value to the business through developing and delivering new IT services
- Managing the expectations and perceptions the business has of IT

Scope of Service Level Management

It has become appallingly obvious that our technology has exceeded our humanity.
– Albert Einstein

The scope of Service Level Management ideally covers every aspect of providing IT services to the business. This includes everything from the initial discussion of how technology can be used in new ways to benefit the business to phasing out services that have served their purpose and reached the end of their useful life.

In addition, Service Level Management addresses any negotiations with customers. Even though the other process areas provide information that is used in the negotiation process, only Service Level Management negotiates the terms of service with customers. Included in negotiations with customers is the presentation of financial data that supports the IT position for recovering costs through either budgeting or charging. Financial Management conducts cost analysis using financial tools such as cost breakdown models and transfers the data to Service Level Management where it is included in a comprehensive negotiation strategy that ensures value to the business in return for providing adequate IT resources.

Service Level Management personnel negotiate with customers. No other process area personnel do this, even though they do provide supporting data for the negotiations.

Keep in mind the distinction between end-users and customers. Service Desk is the single point of contact for end-users while Service Level Management is the primary source of contact for customers.

In this role of customer liaison, Service Level Management is naturally at the top of a pyramid representing the areas of its responsibility. Service Level Management is responsible to the customer for providing the agreed upon services, which naturally leads to Service Level Management taking a coordinating role in the activities and performance of every other process area. ITIL does not set forth a direct hierarchy for the process area relationships, but the scope and responsibility as well as the inputs and outputs of each process area create a sort of natural hierarchy as represented in Figure 9-1.

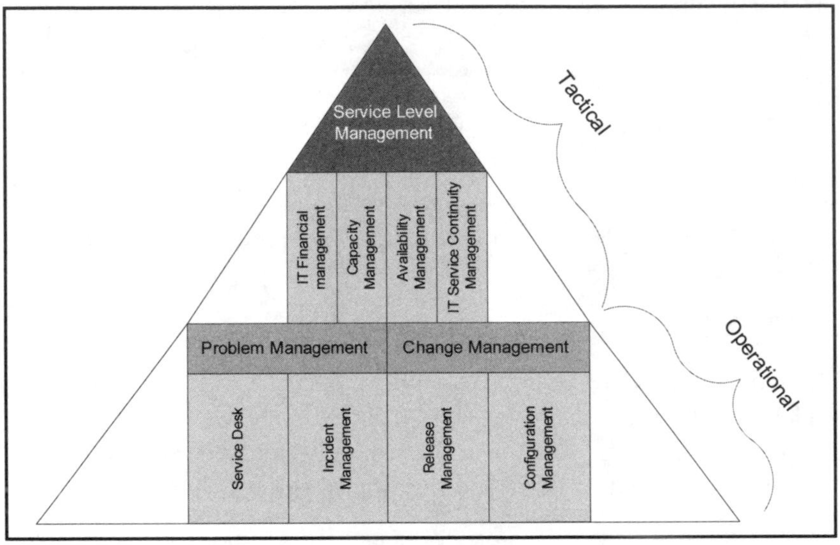

Figure 9-1: Responsibility pyramid

In Figure 9-1 Service Level Management sits at the apex of the pyramid owning responsibility for all IT interaction with the business at the tactical and operational levels. Service Level Management coordinates the activities of the four Service Delivery processes. It also coordinates the operational level processes, which have their own responsibility hierarchy. At the operational level, Problem Management has responsibility for Service Desk and Incident Management, while Change Management has responsibility for Release Management and Configuration Management. Service Desk continues to have responsibility for being the single point of contact for end-users.

Costs vs. Benefits

Not everything that can be counted counts, and not everything that counts can be counted.
– Albert Einstein

The number of services and the levels of service that IT is able to provide are always bounded by the associated costs. IT Service Level Management is responsible for helping customers understand the trade-offs between cost and benefit of any given service or service level. The goal is to enable the business to make informed decisions about which services it requires and what levels of service are justifiable, given the current business environment.

In organizations without strong Service Level Management, IT is often forced to make business decisions without a clear understanding of the business environment and its drivers, which often results in frustration on the part of both the business and IT because the business feels powerless to make service decisions and IT feels that the business is ungrateful for its efforts.

Implementing Service Level Management has up front costs. However, those costs are easily offset by the benefits derived from the improved working relationship between IT and the business. If it is important that IT be seen as a strategic partner to the business, then it is incumbent upon IT to demonstrate that reality by allocating resources and management commitment to both a Service Level Management process and a Service Level Manager.

Some of the costs associated with Service Level Management are:

- Staff costs.
- Accommodation costs.
- Support tool costs.
- Hardware costs.
- Marketing costs.

Some of the benefits of Service Level Management are:

- Improved customer relationship and customer perception of IT.
- Clear roles and responsibilities between IT and its customers and among groups within IT.
- Specific targets for measurement and reporting are agreed upon and communicated.
- IT efforts are more often focused on business priorities.
- Expectations between IT and its customers and among groups within IT are agreed upon and communicated.
- A clear basis is established for measuring performance of suppliers.
- Clearly defined services provide a basis to charge or budget for IT services that are relevant to the customer's business.

The Service Level Management Process

Successful collaborative negotiation lies in finding out what the other side really wants and showing them a way to get it, while you get what you want.
– Herb Cohen

ITIL discusses four major processes within the Service Level Management process:

- Planning the process
- Implementing the process
- Managing the ongoing process
- Periodic reviews

Planning the Process

A good plan today is better than a perfect plan tomorrow.
– General George S. Patton

The following four activity groups fall under planning the process:

- Initial planning activities
- Plan monitoring capabilities.
- Establish initial perception of the services.
- Plan underpinning contracts and operational level agreements.

Initial Planning Activities

The following activities may need to be conducted if Service Level Management is not already in place:

- Appoint a service level manager.
- Produce a mission statement (ITIL recommends following well established project management disciplines.)
- Define objectives and scope of Service Level Management in your organization.
- Initiate an awareness campaign.
- Define roles tasks and responsibilities.
- Quantify activities, resources, funding, and quality criteria.
- Identify risks.
- Plan the service catalog and SLA structure.

- Draft a pilot SLA format.
- Identify support tools particularly for monitoring.
- Set and agree upon incident priority levels and escalation paths with customers and internal and external providers.

The communication path among service level targets and detailed triggers and escalation points for Incident Management and the Service Desk is not provided in significant detail within the ITIL text. I am of the opinion that Service Level Management provides the service targets to Problem Management and works with Problem Management to ensure that an adequate plan is in place to ensure that the targets can be met. This plan should document the specific triggers and escalation points that will be provided to the Service Desk and Incident Management.

Since neither Service Level Management nor Problem Management have sufficient insight and expertise to do this alone, the two must work together. It also makes sense to have Problem Management monitor and adjust triggers and escalation points on a day-to-day basis and report the impacts to Service Level Management on a periodic basis.

Plan Monitoring Capabilities

In order for processes and services to be managed and optimized, there must be a feedback loop that provides management information regarding the functioning of the process or service. This requires monitoring the process or service in appropriate ways to ensure that it is meeting the stated goal in the most effective and efficient manner. From an ITIL or quality perspective, the success of the process or service is measured at the point where the output of the process or service is consumed. Within the ITIL framework, this means that services are measured from the end-user and customer perspective or on an end-to-end basis.

Monitoring on an end-to-end basis requires monitoring every component in a service from the server to the workstation and requires monitoring the execution of service tasks. IT must be able to verify that each component in the service is functioning to specifications. However, monitoring just the components is not sufficient. Monitoring should simulate service functionality from end-to-end ensuring that from an end-user's perspective the service is providing its expected results.

Plan Initial Perception of the Services

We learned that the Service Desk is directly responsible for end-user perception of IT and indirectly responsible for customer perception. Now, we learn that Service Level Management is directly responsible for customer perception of IT, which is influenced by end-user perceptions. Therefore, Service Level Management will be very interested in monitoring Service Desk performance.

Always remember that customers have budget or influence sufficient to secure services from IT while end-users are the consumers of those services. The needs and perspectives of the two groups are very different and require different approaches from IT in order to meet their needs. Customers will at times be end-users when they are consuming IT services and interfacing with the Service Desk. During these times, their concerns and needs are end-user concerns and needs.

Service Level Management should make every effort to develop a baseline of understanding for the initial perception of new services. This will enable IT to paint a "before and after" picture once Service Level Management is firmly established. Part of that picture should include the lack of adequate capability to measure perception prior to implementation, which represents a significant deficiency in IT management's ability to control or predict a major environmental factor.

Many managers, after implementing improvements, will say that they cannot demonstrate improvements from implementation because there were no measurements beforehand. Responding in this way misses the point.

Improvements can be measured in terms of identifying previously unidentified risks and providing for mitigation and contingencies. Improvements can also be measured in terms of moving the organization from a point of minimal or no precise data upon which to make business decisions to a point where informed business decisions can be made.

Too often technical people are limited by their technical measuring experience and miss valuable measurements that are not precise or numerical. From a business perspective, moving from no informed decision making capability to some informed decision making capability has significant value, even if measuring the value in hard terms is difficult.

The improvement picture should be completed by showing how the new capabilities allow IT management to measure and report customer perception of IT following implementation; therefore, providing the ability to predict and positively influence a major environmental factor for IT success.

Plan Underpinning Contracts and Operational Level Agreements

Plans need to be made for evaluating and implementing or improving UCs and OLAs in support of new SLA targets. Service level agreements are interdependent rather than stand-alone documents. They depend on operational level agreements that set targets among internal IT groups for providing services in support of end-user facing services. OLAs are typically less formal than SLAs and provide for more technical detail.

Often, services are dependent on outside vendors for parts of their functionality. For SLA targets to be achievable, the underpinning contracts with those vendors must support the SLA targets. Underpinning contracts are legal documents that require more extensive due diligence before implementing. These contracts will contain many of the same elements as SLAs such as service level targets, but they must be recognized as legally binding documents.

Implementing the Process

A journey of a thousand miles begins with a single step.
– Confucius

There are a number of activities involved in implementing the Service Level Management process:

Produce a Service Catalog – A service catalog is a document that lists all customer-facing services, the available service levels, and the costs at each level. It has many uses in the organization from helping with customer negotiations and business impact analysis to helping the Service Desk do its job.

The service catalog may contain supporting details such as the sub-services that support customer facing services. Having the capability to present visually the entire service chain and the costs of delivering each sub-service at the required level reassures the business that IT understands its costs and can justify them appropriately. This level of documentation provides significant negotiating leverage and should pay for itself by helping to secure additional resources from the business. The individual services should be entered as CIs in the CMDB, allowing incidents, problems, and changes to be linked with specific services. This also helps identify operational costs for existing services.

By entering the services into the CMDB as CIs, the organization has the ability to present the service catalog in many different ways depending on the audience. For negotiations with the customer, a compact representation of the available services, associated service levels, and costs is appropriate. This presentation may even show a graphical representation of the service chain with a table of supporting detail. However, for end-users, the service catalog may need to be represented from the component perspective. For instance, when an incident relates to a specific CI the Service Desk needs to quickly identify any customer-facing services that are dependent on that CI so that incident category and priority can be accurately assigned.

Expectation Management – How can satisfaction be determined?
Satisfaction = expectation – perception

If there are no costs associated with service provision, customers (as rational beings) will expect IT to provide the highest levels of service possible regardless of need. This system is ineffective because it ensures a high cost for all services. The ability to align costs to delivered services provides the customer with the ability to manage their own desired levels of service; at the same time, it allows IT an effective means to ensure that the business provides for the true cost of service. Implementing a charging system aligned with services where the business actually pays IT directly for service provision is an option that some organizations may choose.

Charging is an optional concept in ITIL. Business culture usually dictates whether business units charge one another directly for services or whether they simply allocate budgets. Whichever method is used, IT should match what the other business units are doing. Regardless, IT should be able to demonstrate its costs in relation to services and customers in support of the budgeting and negotiating processes.

Satisfaction is a combination of hard and soft measures. Expectation can be a hard measure defined in service targets and, at the same time, be a soft measure determined by the human interaction between customers and Service Level Management. Much hard work in defining and achieving hard measure targets can result in poor end-user/customer satisfaction if soft measures are not also improved. This occurs when perceptions do not match reality. To ensure satisfaction, IT must recognize the importance of ensuring that hard and soft measures align.

Hard measures are those measures where easily quantifiable numbers can be gathered such as response times, resolution of incidents at first contact, etc. Soft measures are those measures that are subjective in nature such as courteousness, staff knowledge, empathy, etc. When hard and soft measures are out of alignment, this is an indication that communication is ineffective.

Expectations can be set through service level targets and supported through communication. However, more still needs to be done. Perception is an important part of this equation and it is primarily a soft measure affected by how well IT communicates with its customers. Reporting is discussed in more detail in the Availability Management chapter, but essentially IT must get better at communicating its successes. It must also get better at speaking in terms its end-users and customers care about and understand. If this is not done IT will fail to meet the perception side of the satisfaction equation and the business will not be satisfied with IT performance no matter how hard IT works.

Establish Service Level Requirements (SLR) and Draft SLAs – ITIL introduces a term, service level requirement (SLR), that identifies the requirements a customer has for a given service. Often there is a difference in the targets identified in service level requirements and the targets agreed upon in service level agreements. There are a number of reasons for this:

> Many organizations do not have a well-defined system for aligning costs to services. Therefore, customers often have very little perspective on the costs involved in delivering a service at any given service level. This leads customers to demand the maximum level of service available. In these organizations, political negotiation is required to keep costs under control.
>
> Often with new services, customers are not fully aware of all of their service needs, and their requirements for services grow as they gain experience.
>
> Service level requirements define the desired state, while service level agreements define the proven to be achievable state. Often lengthy and difficult improvements in technology and processes are required for IT to prove it can deliver a service at a given service level. Only after the capability is demonstrated should IT provide a guarantee in the form of an SLA.

Wording of SLAs – SLAs should be clear and concise with no room for ambiguity, and common language should be preferred over legal terminology.

> The basic assumption when using legal terminology in a document is that there will be conflict that requires third-party intervention. The idea of Service Level Management is to build working relationships with the business, not a legal or conflict-based relationship. Therefore, common language should be preferred.

Reviews should be conducted by disinterested parties to ensure clarity of wording for those not involved in the drafting. Often two parties deeply involved in negotiations come to common understanding about parts of the document, but the language in the document does not reflect that common understanding to "third parties." It is considered a best practice to have disinterested third parties review the document and articulate to the negotiating parties how they interpret the document.

Internationalization is also a critical concern. Language and cultural differences often prove to be large stumbling blocks. Ensuring that parties from each affected region are part of the process will help with this concern.

Seeking Agreement – Service Level Management is about providing services and service levels required by the business at costs that are justifiable to the business.

This requires establishing working relationships at multiple levels between IT and the customer/user base. SLAs should represent the culmination of a successful working partnership between IT and the business.

The SLA should be achievable at the quoted cost and meet the levels of service that the business requires at that cost.

Adversarial relationships are often the result of frustration on both sides and derive from a broken or non-existent Service Level Management process.

Build a good process and be patient. Relationships take time and dedication.

Establishing Monitoring Capabilities – Monitoring of the service is crucial to all parties involved.

Monitoring should be conducted from end to end.

Its scope should be agreed upon by all parties.

Reviewing UCs and OLAs – This topic is discussed in detail later in this chapter.

Defining Reporting and Review Procedures – One of the keys to changing the perception of IT by customers is to change the way reporting is done. Many organizations do the majority of their reporting on an "exception" basis. They only report when things go wrong and fail to highlight the good work that is done every day. The majority of measures and terms used by IT serve to highlight exceptions. Reporting should be conducted on a regularly scheduled basis and this opportunity should always be utilized to highlight the good work IT is doing. This supports the critical Service Level Management responsibility of managing perception

Publicizing the existence of SLAs – Awareness campaigns are a critical component of any process-based approach to implementing process improvements. Stakeholders need to be aware of what is taking place, key people need to be sold on the value, and key executives need to openly show their support and commitment. It must be well understood that the organization is committed to gaining the value potential that Service Level Management represents.

Planning the Service Level Agreement Structure

Wise Man: One who sees the storm coming before the clouds appear.
– Elbert Hubbard

There are three kinds of SLA structures defined by ITIL:

1. **Service Based** – This is an SLA covering one service that is the same for the entire organization. It is effective when the requirements for the service are the same for all organizations or departments. It is also effective when the difference in cost for providing the highest required level of service versus the lowest required level of service is insignificant. In this scenario, the highest required level of service would be provided to all, simply to avoid the management costs of carrying two service levels for such things as negotiations and documentation. This is often the way messaging services are provided when high speed, reliable network connections are available to all departments.

2. **Customer Based** – In this scenario one agreement for each given customer group covers all their services. Agreements may differ between customer groups. This scenario is very simple for the customers, but may be costly or difficult for IT to provide. This is often the way messaging services are provided when some departments have limited network connections.

3. **Multi-level SLAs** – This scenario allows for a tiered solution that provides for as many nested levels of SLAs as is needed. ITIL identifies three tiers under which service level agreements may be defined. At the corporate level, generic services are provided at the same level of service for everyone, while other services will require an added level of detail at the customer level with SLAs defined for each customer group or collection of groups having the same requirements. The third level is where individual services within a customer group are provided with a unique level of service.

Establishing Monitoring Capabilities

It takes humility to seek feedback. It takes wisdom to understand it, analyze it, and appropriately act on it.
– Stephen R. Covey

SLAs should only include those items that can be effectively monitored and measured at a commonly agreed upon point. Inclusion of items that cannot be effectively monitored almost always results in disputes and eventual loss of faith in the Service Level Management process.

It is essential that monitoring matches the customer's true perception of the service. A service that is available only to the edge of the data center and not to the end-user is not a complete service and provides little value to the business. Monitoring of services must show the service from an end-to-end or value perspective. Monitoring must also detect when failure of a component recorded at the Service Desk results in failure of a service and potentially of an SLA. Further, it should indicate how many end-users are potentially impacted by the failure. This will determine the impact and possibly the urgency of a given incident.

This capability requires a well-functioning CMDB and the ability to connect incidents with both components and services. Therefore, it is very important that appropriate processes and procedures are in place to ensure that the Service Desk associates incidents with the correct CI. If this is not done, reporting may indicate SLA breaches where none actually occur or it may indicate no breaches when they do occur. It is also critical that SLA information, such as riggers and escalations match between the Service Level Management and incident/problem recording systems.

There are a number of important 'soft' issues such as customer perception that cannot be monitored by technical or procedural means and may not match 'hard' monitoring. For instance, even when there have been a number of reported service failures the customers/end-users may still have a positive perception of IT performance. The opposite may also happen when the service is performing normally, but customers/end-users still feel dissatisfied. These types of disconnects primarily occur because of human interaction between end-users and the Service Desk or customers and Service Level Management. In these situations, perception often outweighs the facts and human errors taint the perception of IT.

Perception is reality. It is a common misconception that we react to events in life, but in reality, we react to our perception of events. For example, let's say a car pulls out in front of you and cuts you off. How do you react? Are you angry, scared, oblivious, or resigned? As you read this, many of you are certain that everyone feels the way you do and cannot fathom that there is another possible reaction. In this situation, you do not react to the car cutting you off; you react to the meaning you attribute to the car cutting you off. If you think of it as an aggressive act, you will react in anger. If you think of it as inevitable because there are poor drivers out there, you are more likely to feel resigned. We react to our perceptions not to events.

How does this translate to IT? Customers and end-users base their opinions about IT on their perceptions of IT regardless of the actual events that occur. Therefore, IT personnel must make establishing relationships with their customers and end-users priority in order to affect perception. Good salesmen succeed because they maintain relationships with their customers, and those customers prefer to buy from someone they know. They can get products anywhere. They buy because the customer perceives value in buying from the salesman they know. When IT actively promotes positive relationships with their customers and end-users, perception of IT is positive, resulting in success for both IT and the business.

– Christine Belaire, Ph.D.

Given the importance of soft issues, the question arises; how can soft issues be measured? The simple answer is to ask the customer or end-user what their perception is. Measuring soft issues, however, is as much an art as it is science. Political pollsters, the masters of this art, are famous for asking the same question in slightly different ways and getting completely different results. They are also famous for selecting the wrong group of people to ask.

Measuring soft issues will take continuous effort over time but it is vital for the long-term success of IT. One way to increase the objectivity of these measures over time is to set targets for soft issues that can be quantified and improved. Some examples of these targets are:

- Unacceptable performance
- Poor performance
- Acceptable performance

- Good performance
- Excellent performance

Reviewing UCs and OLAs

Watch your thoughts; they become words.
Watch your words; they become actions.
Watch your actions; they become habits.
Watch your habits; they become character.
Watch your character; it becomes your destiny.
– Frank Outlaw

There are three basic types of service dependency:

1. Services can be dependent upon multiple groups within IT. These groups define agreements among themselves to deliver services at levels sufficient to meet the service targets documented in the SLA with the customer. These agreements between IT groups are less formal than SLAs and are called operational level agreements.

2. Services can be dependent on only one group within IT so that only the formal SLA with the customer is required to deliver the required levels of service.

3. Services can be dependent on outside suppliers. In this scenario, contracts are required to define the level of service to be delivered by the outside contractor. These are called Underpinning Contracts in ITIL. The underpinning contracts are legal documents that set legal penalties for noncompliance with agreed terms. Part of the agreed terms will be a defined set of service targets.

It is important that these agreements are understood and reviewed regularly by all stakeholders to ensure that changes at one level are reflected at all levels.

ITIL provides three documents with specific names, each with a specific purpose. Each document carries with it a requirement for a certain level of detail and due diligence. When lumping these three documents under one term, SLA, as is commonly done today, mistakes can easily be made in applying the appropriate level of due diligence. These mistakes can be very costly for the unlucky companies that make them. Having each document type clearly labeled makes it much harder to make a due diligence mistake, while it also clarifies and simplifies communication.

Operational level agreements (OLA) are the least formal of the three documents. They apply only among groups within the IT department itself. They serve to set agreements for the delivery of sub-services. Disputes among parties rise only to the level of the CIO and incur no legal penalties.

Service level agreements (SLA) are more formal than OLA. They apply between IT and other organizations within the same company. They serve to set agreements for the delivery of customer-facing services. Disputes among parties rise only to the CEO or the company Board of Directors and do not have legal penalties.

Underpinning contracts are formal. They use legal language and should be reviewed by the company's legal council. They apply between the company and another legal entity. They set agreements for the delivery of both customer-facing services and sub-services. Disputes between parties rise to the governing court system.

The Ongoing Process

The great thing, and the hard thing, is to stick to things when you have outlived the first interest, and not yet got the second, which comes with a sort of mastery.
– Janet Erskine Stuart

There are four key activities that support the ongoing process of Service Level Management:

1. Monitoring and reporting
2. Service review meetings
3. Service improvement programs
4. Maintenance of SLAs, UCs, and OLAs

Monitoring and Reporting – Service Level Management must monitor services against SLAs and report to the customer on a regular basis demonstrating how well IT is performing against the SLA targets.

Service Level Agreement Monitoring (SLAM) Report – The SLAM report is a very useful tool for reporting service level achievements. It is designed primarily for customers and is easily understandable at a glance. One important benefit of the SLAM report is that it effectively represents the good work that IT is doing, represented by the predominance of green in the report.

The rows indicate different service level targets and the columns indicate reporting periods. The colors indicate target achievements for each period:

- Green (light gray) = target met
- Yellow (medium gray) = potential to miss target
- Red (dark gray) = target missed

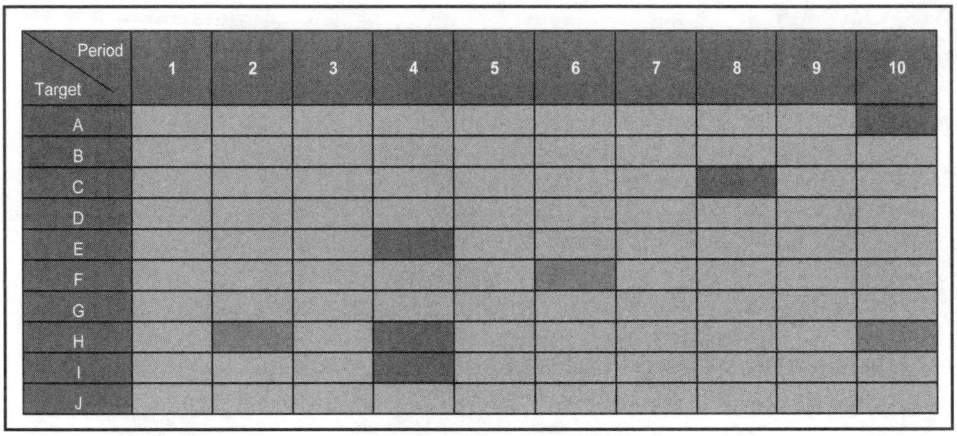

Figure 9-2: SLAM report

Service review meetings – Regular service review meetings should be held with the customer to discuss current and future service provisions. These meetings should examine failures to meet SLA targets and the changes IT is implementing to ensure that targets are met in the future. They should also examine changing business needs and the potential for new service needs.

Service improvement program – Service Level Management is tasked with ensuring that resources are allocated and utilized to continuously improve the levels of service delivered, while reducing the associated costs. This is accomplished through formal specialized projects called service improvement programs (SIP).

Maintenance of SLAs, Contracts and OLAs – The business constantly changes, IT capabilities grow, and costs for providing IT services change over time. This requires that service level management constantly review and adjust the agreements that it maintains to ensure optimum service delivery at minimum costs.

Service Level Agreements and Key Targets

All winning teams are goal-oriented. Teams like these win consistently because everyone connected with them concentrates on specific objectives. They go about their business with blinders on; nothing will distract them from achieving their aims.
– Lou Holtz

This is a list of common contents and key targets for service level agreements:

Introduction - provides a context within which the SLA should be evaluated

Service hours - indicates when the requirements of the SLA must be met. From an IT perspective, they indicate windows of opportunity for maintenance and troubleshooting.

Availability - indicates the level of availability to be achieved and the parameters of measurement

Reliability - indicates the quantity of failures that are tolerated

Support - indicates the level of support available, the means of reaching support, the allowable response times, and the agreed upon hours of support

These are by no means all of the contents that you might see within SLAs, but they are some of the most common. The items elaborated upon are core contents that should be in practically every SLA you encounter. Other contents and key targets are:

- Throughput.
- Transaction response times.
- Batch turnaround times.
- Targets for handling changes.
- IT service continuity and security.
- Details of charging.
- Service reporting and reviewing expectations.
- Performance incentives/penalties.

The Service Level Manager

Superior leaders get things done with very little motion. They impart instruction not through many words, but through a few deeds. They keep informed about everything but interfere hardly at all. They are catalysts, and though things would not get done as well if they were not there, when they succeed they take no credit. And, because they take no credit, credit never leaves them.
– Lao-Tzu

Service Level Management acts as a "go between" for customers and IT, serving as both a customer advocate and an IT advocate while ensuring that expectations and perceptions on both sides are managed. Accordingly, the service level manager needs to possess a high level of diplomatic skills and the ability to communicate effectively within both the business and IT arenas. The natural tendency for each group is to think that the service level manager works for the other group. An individual whose skills are primarily technical in nature will have difficulty managing this type of situation whereas a true diplomat will fit easily into both groups serving to bring the groups closer together.

Conclusion

Service Level Management has responsibility for all the other process areas in ITIL and is directly responsible for customer perception of IT. It is the only process area that negotiates with customers. It utilizes service level agreements between IT and the business, operational level agreements among groups within IT, and underpinning contracts with outside legal entities to provide assurances to the business that services will be delivered as agreed. It provides an appropriate structured approach for service level agreements. In short, Service Level Management ensures that all operational and tactical processes within IT are aligned in support of business needs.

Exam Preparation Questions

1. What is the goal of Service Level Management?
2. What are the costs and five benefits of Service Level Management?
3. What are the four stages of the Service Level Management process?
4. Service Level Management is primarily responsible for negotiating with which group?
5. What are the three listed SLA structures?
6. What type of wording should be utilized in SLAs and OLAs?
7. What type of wording should be avoided in SLAs and OLAs?
8. Monitoring should be matched to what?
9. How are soft issues measured?
10. Why are soft issues important?
11. Where are measurements taken to determine success of a process or service?
12. What is Service Level Management directly responsible for?
13. How is the service catalog used?
14. How is satisfaction determined?
15. What is the difference between SLRs and SLAs?
16. What are five of the most common service level targets found in SLAs?
17. Be able to define the following in ITIL terms:
    1. SLA
    2. SLR
    3. OLA
    4. UC

5. Service catalog
6. Service review meeting
7. Service improvement program

10

Financial Management for IT Services

Introduction

Every decision must be based on these principles: "Can the cost really be lowered?" and "Can this action help the company's overall performance?"
– Taiichi Ohno

Financial Management for IT Services is responsible for ensuring that IT can demonstrate that the money devoted to it is managed well. But more than that, finance is the language of business. To understand business, to communicate with the business, and to build relationships with the business requires a fluency in the language of business. Introducing Financial Management for IT Services to the ITIL mix ensures that IT is managed in a manner that is familiar to business and that can be described in business terms. It is a key element in the formula that delivers business-aligned IT services.

Every communication channel with business customers, to be effective, must resonate with the language of business, Finance. Customers have limited budgets that must be used to maximum advantage. IT often takes a large portion of that budget without clearly articulating the advantage provided. This leads to the business asking IT to provide more just to ensure that they are getting the best deal possible. Then IT finds itself in the role of continuously asking for more money to effectively get the job done. IT could go a long way towards ending this cycle by simply understanding that the behavior comes from a need to receive recognizable value for money spent.

ITIL provides the tools for effectively communicating value for money spent in the form of Financial Management for IT Services, the name given to the process responsible for:

Budgeting – The process for predicting and controlling the spending of money within the organization, it consists of a periodic negotiation cycle to set budgets, and the day-to-day monitoring of the current budgets.

IT Accounting – The set of processes that enable the IT organization to account fully for the way its money is spent, particularly the ability to identify costs by customer, service, or activity.

Charging – The set of processes required to bill customers for the services supplied to them.

Goal of Financial Management

The goal of Financial Management is to provide cost-effective stewardship of the IT assets and the financial resources used in providing IT services.

Under ITIL, Financial Management is concerned with sound stewardship of the IT assets and financial resources used in providing IT services. In its advanced capabilities, Financial Management is involved in helping Service Level Management, Availability Management, Service Continuity Management, and Capacity Management transform the way IT and the business communicate.

The primary way it achieves this is by bringing the full power of the accounting profession to bear on associating costs of IT service provision with customers and IT services. In other words, IT leverages the professional skills of the accounting department to transform the way it communicates with the other business departments. This enables IT to provide the business with the information it needs to make sound business decisions; a transformation that relieves the business decision making burden from IT and frees IT from taking the heat for those decisions.

Why Financial Management

There is no such thing as a free lunch.
– Anonymous

Financial Management for IT Services is an integral part of service management. It provides the essential management information to ensure that services are run efficiently, economically, and cost effectively.

An effective Financial Management system does the following:

- It drives down long-term costs.
- It associates costs to services so that business is empowered to make decisions.
- It helps IT demonstrate value added.
- It provides for better total cost of ownership (TCO) & return on investment (ROI) calculations as operating costs are quantified.
- It helps IT demonstrate value for the money the business pays.
- It causes the business to take an active role in limiting demand by making the costs of services and service levels visible.
- It provides senior management with better assurances that the IT function is under control and meeting business needs.
- It helps change managers to better understand the operational lifecycle costs of new projects.

Responsibilities

The price of excellence is discipline. The cost of mediocrity is disappointment.
– William Arthur Ward

IT Financial Management has certain core responsibilities that may be reflected in an organization's goals for implementing IT Financial Management. These core responsibilities are:

- Enable the organization to account fully for the expenditure on IT services and to attribute these costs to the services delivered.
- Assist management decisions on IT investment by supporting detailed business cases for change.
- Control and manage overall IT budget and enable fair and equitable recovery of costs, by charging for provision of IT services when appropriate.

Financial Management Activities

Finance is the art of passing currency from hand to hand until it finally disappears.
– Robert W. Sarnoff

The major Financial Management activities are:

- Budgeting.
- Accounting.
- Charging.

Financial Management typically receives documentation of business needs and requirements from Service Level Management. In return, Financial Management provides budgeting, accounting, and charging information back to Service Level Management, so that it can manage customer expectations and negotiate services.

Service Level Management negotiates with customers. IT Financial Management identifies costs, proposes prices for services, and provides the appropriate financial data to support negotiations.

Some of the responsibilities of these activities are:

Budgeting & Accounting:

- Forecast money required to run IT services for a given period.
- Ensure that the actual expenditure can be compared with the predicted expenditure at any point.
- Account for the money spent in IT services in a given period.
- Calculate the cost of IT service provision.

Charging:

- Recover the cost of the IT services from the customers of the service.
- Operate the IT services as a business unit, if required.

Accounting terms:

- **Depreciation** is the measure of the reduction in the useful economic life of a capital item. It takes into account the current value of the asset, the expected remaining length of life, and any residual value of the asset at the end of its useful life. It is "writing off" the cost of an item over multiple years primarily for tax purposes.)

Common Depreciation Methods include:

•Straight-line.
•Reducing balance.
•By usage.

- **Differential charging** is a charging policy aimed either at dampening demand for a scarce or expensive resource or encouraging the use of spare capacity. It is a charging policy that aims to manage the amount of a service that customers use, i.e., encouraging them to use more or use less by setting an appropriate price. (See also: Demand Management in the Capacity Management chapter.)

It is important to remember the differences between differential charging as a charging policy that is part of Financial Management and Demand Management that is an activity in Capacity Management. Differential charging is one method of practicing demand management. Another method would be by management directive.

Charging Policies

Don't confuse "value" with "price."

When a consumer buys a product, he does so because that product has a certain value to him.
– Taiichi Ohno

Charging policy terms are an important part of business language in which IT managers should be fluent. Even if the organization does not do formal "charge back" to the business units, the ability to communicate with the business in these terms will increase positive perception of IT. It will also help the business feel that the price they pay for IT services is justified and comparable to anything they could receive from another source.

There are many reasons for implementing a charging policy, but similar benefits can be gained in organizations that do not choose to directly charge back the cost of IT to their customers. Many organizations choose to demonstrate costs per customer or service during budgeting without ever formally charging the business; achieving similar benefits without the added complexity.

A service has "value" only if the customer deems it worthy of their money. Product-based businesses have a built in mechanism for providing value (i.e. the tangible product itself). However, service-based businesses have more of a disadvantage because their product is not tangible. Service managers must work harder to create the "image of value" for their customers. Charging a monetary amount for service is one method of assigning value to service.

Value is an abstract concept that fluctuates according to who perceives the value. An item that is free may be perceived as having little value, whereas a more expensive item may be perceived as more valuable regardless of the true value. The service provider assigns value to the service based on his/her perception of training required, time allocated, resources available, etc. However, the client assigns value according to his/her need, potential downtime, cost/benefit ratio, etc. Creating value in the eyes of the customer is about creating an image that reflects the customer's perceptions.

People respect what they think is valuable. In any business, but particularly in a service business, we must define how our services provide value to the customer. If perception is unmanaged, customers will assign value based on their own perceptions, which makes achieving customer satisfaction a roll-of-the-dice. Charging for service assigns a monetary value, which begins the process, but it must be followed up by clearly defined value expectations so that the customer perception of that monetary value equals that of the service provider.

In the past, IT has been viewed as a product-based business, which probably contributed to the low value perception at times. Customers may have identified value with IT products (i.e. hardware, software, etc.) and discounted IT service. More effectively conceptualizing IT as a service business allows IT to define its value based on service and product. When IT takes an active role in defining its value, customers have a higher value perception of IT. Therefore, sound business decisions can be made based on a unified value for service.

– Christine Belaire, Ph.D.

Charging customers for use of IT services is a cultural decision. If other parts of the organization practice charge backs then it may make sense for IT to also practice charging. However, if no other parts of the organization practice charging then it is probably wiser for IT simply to demonstrate that it understands its costs sufficiently to support charging without formally doing so.

These are the five charging policies identified by ITIL:

1. **Cost** - Price = cost
2. **Cost-plus -** Price = cost ± X%

3. **Going rate -** Price is comparable with other internal departments' costs within the organization or with similar organizations.
4. **Market rate -** Price matches that charged by external suppliers.
5. **Fixed price -** A set price is agreed upon for a set period with the customer, based on anticipated usage.

Cost Categorizations

That which costs little is less valued.
– Miguel de Cervantes Saavedra

Think of cost categorizations as 'buckets' into which money is placed. In an effort to understand and demonstrate where money goes, accounting has developed these buckets as a way to categorize expenditures. Every cost to IT is allocated to three of the six buckets:

1. **Capital or Operational -** A cost is either a capital cost or an operational cost. This means IT either spent money to purchase a piece of equipment or the money went to day-to-day expenses for running IT.

2. **Direct or Indirect -** The cost is then either a direct cost which means the cost was either all for one customer, customer group, or service; or the cost was an indirect cost and must be shared through some formula with more than one customer, customer group, or service.

3. **Fixed or Variable -** The cost is then either a fixed cost which means that it is the same from period to period, such as rent; or it is a variable cost which is subject to change from period to period, such as utility costs or travel expenses.

IT people categorize things like data all the time. In a database, a data field is either text or numeric, fixed width or variable, integer, or floating point. These distinctions have great meaning to technical people, but are often meaningless to business people. Likewise, accounting terms have great meaning to business people. As a services organization, IT must be respectful and knowledgeable of business language.

Service Cost Model

Education costs money, but then so does ignorance.
– Sir Moser Claus

A cost model uses accounting terminology and knowledge to show in detail where the money goes. Figure 10-1, an example of a service cost model, shows expenditures in relation to defined services. Cost models allow IT to reflect costs in relation to business activities. This in turn helps IT to become more aligned with the business.

Across the top of Figure 10-1, we see all the cost elements (sources of expenditures) associated with a given service.

- Hardware
- Software
- Equipment
- Accommodation
- External Service
- Transfer

Some of these costs can be capital expenditures such as hardware, software, and accommodation. Others can be operational such as employment, external services, and accommodation costs (electricity, utilities, versus rent). Some can even be both depending on their use and their relative cost such as accommodation and software.

Some of the costs are directly attributable to this particular service (direct costs). Some of the costs are shared or indirect, but easily divided (absorbed indirect costs) such as dividing rent by amount of floor space used. Other costs are indirect but not so easily divided (unabsorbed indirect costs) such as electricity, utilities, and insurance. These unabsorbed costs of service have to be divided in a subjective manner that usually requires negotiation between all the parties involved and a management decision.

To achieve the total cost for a service, first combine the direct costs and the absorbed indirect costs. Then allocate an appropriate portion of the unabsorbed indirect costs to this service and combine all three costs together. This produces a total cost for the IT service in question. The total cost with the detailed cost structure can then be used to demonstrate to the business where their money has gone, and to help them feel that the cost is justified.

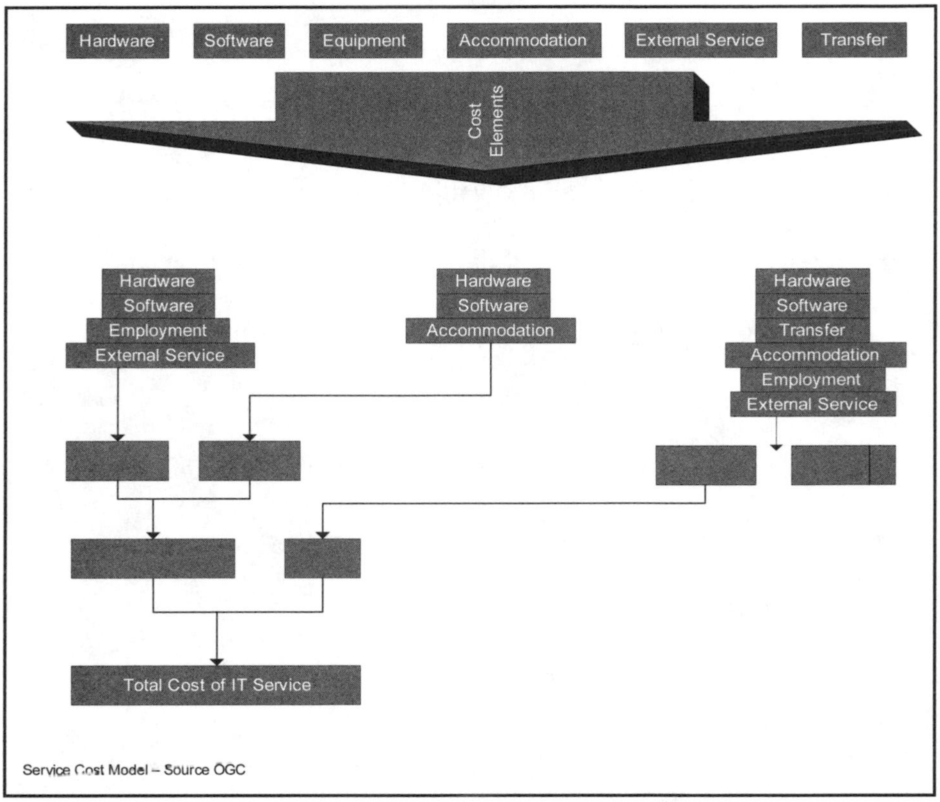

Figure 10-1: Service cost model

Conclusion

IT Financial Management is responsible for budgeting, accounting, and charging and is concerned with sound stewardship of financial assets and resources used in provision of IT services. The primary reason for practicing Financial Management for IT Services is to justify the cost of providing IT services to the business. The basic language of accounting is familiar to most business managers and is a language that IT managers must understand in order to effectively manage business perceptions of IT. The final element to understand is how accounting uses cost models to systematically assign costs to customers, services, or activities in an effort to rationalize expenditures.

Exam Preparation Questions

1. What is the goal of Financial Management?
2. Complete this statement: ITIL Financial Management for IT services is the name given to the process responsible for ____________, _____________, and _______________ .
3. List five things an effective Financial Management system does.
4. What are the three core responsibilities of Financial Management?
5. What are the three major Financial Management activities?
6. Why is differential charging used?
7. What are the five charging policies identified by ITIL? Define each.
8. What are the six cost categorizations and why are they used?
9. What is a cost model used for?
10. Be able to define the following in ITIL terms:
    1. Depreciation
    2. Differential charging
    3. Cost model
    4. Direct cost
    5. Indirect cost
    6. Absorbed indirect cost
    7. Un-absorbed indirect cost

11

Capacity Management

Introduction

They who know how to employ opportunities will often find that they can create them; and what we can achieve depends less on the amount of time we possess than on the use we make of our time.
– John Stuart Mill

Capacity Management is concerned with ensuring that an appropriate level of capacity exists in all resources required to support IT services. This includes technical concerns such as network nodes and bandwidth; as well as people issues, such as technical skill sets and staffing levels. It is intimately involved with forward business planning and ensures that IT is able to support business activities—both today and into the future—at levels of service and costs that are acceptable to the business.

ITIL Capacity Management ensures that all required resources are available as needed, so that capacity emergencies are avoided. 'As needed' means that equipment is not purchased before it is required or at the last minute resulting in lower costs overall.

Goal of Capacity Management

The goal of Capacity Management is to understand the future business requirements (the required service delivery), the organization's operation (the current service delivery), the IT infrastructure (the means of service delivery), and to ensure that all current and future capacity and performance aspects of the business requirements are provided cost effectively.

Capacity Management is all about ensuring that IT plans for and manages the capacity requirements for IT services in direct collaboration with business planning. There is often significant lead time involved in upgrading IT infrastructure to meet the changing demands of business. If IT and the business are not in constant communication about the business environment and business planning, then the business may be unable to meet its goals as it is forced to wait on IT to catch up. At the very least, IT will be forced to expend more resources on catching up than it would if it were involved in planning from the beginning.

By managing capacity in a holistic manner and by planning capacity needs in lockstep with business planning, IT maximizes capacity and minimizes costs.

Capacity Management and the Business

Planning is the process by which profitable growth is sought and attained in a changing and uncertain world.
– Anonymous

Capacity Management is intimately involved in all levels of business planning. At the highest level, business strategy planning, Capacity Management provides information to the business about the level of IT capacity required and the potential technology costs involved in pursuing any given business strategy. Capacity Management also updates the business on trends in IT technology that may impact capacity capabilities and costs.

At the business plan level, specific requirements for head count, transactions, mergers, acquisitions, and any number of business needs are defined, and expectations are set. This information is critical for IT to begin actively planning, purchasing, and adjusting current capacity capabilities.

By utilizing information from business strategy planning and detailed business planning, IT develops an IT strategy to meet business expectations. IT then creates specific plans to implement the IT strategy and begins making the necessary changes through the Change Management process.

Sub - Processes

Almost all quality improvement comes via simplification of design, manufacturing... layout, processes, and procedures.
– Tom Peters

Capacity Management is broken down into three primary sub-processes, which are defined by the scope of their activities.

Business Capacity Management

It is the responsibility of business capacity management to ensure that the future business requirements for IT services are considered, planned for, and implemented in a timely fashion. This can be achieved by using the existing data on current resource utilization to trend, forecast, and model future requirements. Future requirements come from business plans outlining the need for new services and needed improvements or growth in existing services. To be successful at Business Capacity Management, IT must build effective working relationships with the business at all levels.

Service Capacity Management

The focus of service capacity management is on the services that end-users utilize to perform their roles on a daily basis. The view of this sub-process is decidedly focused on the end-to-end service as a whole as opposed to the traditional IT focus on infrastructure components. IT must first look at the overall service to determine the business needs for a particular service versus the capacity to deliver that service before taking a detailed look at the required infrastructure components. Otherwise, IT risks investing resources on IT components that do not materially impact service provision. Such investments do not provide measurable value to the business. When IT views Capacity Management from a services perspective, it naturally becomes more aligned with business needs.

Resource Capacity Management

The focus of resource capacity management is component management, which is the traditional IT view. It is responsible for ensuring that all components that support services are monitored and measured and that projects are conducted to improve component capacity in support of service needs. This structured approach to Capacity Management leads naturally to a more business aligned approach for IT. It also provides a very effective method for prioritizing IT investments based on the most important business needs.

Resource Capacity Management for the most part is performed much as IT has been performing general Capacity Management for many years. The difference between the traditional IT approach and the IT Service Management approach is that Resource Capacity Management efforts are now targeted directly to those component improvements that have the most positive impact to the business. This is accomplished by focusing Capacity Management goals into three distinct hierarchical areas:

1. **Strategy** - business capacity management
2. **Tactics** - service capacity management
3. **Operations** – resource capacity management

Activities in Capacity Management

There are no secrets to success. It is the result of preparation, hard work, and learning from failure.
– Colin Powell

Figure 11-1 shows the major activities within Capacity Management and their relationships to the sub-processes and the Capacity Management database. The activities shown are:

- The Iterative Activities:
  - Monitoring
  - Analysis
  - Tuning
  - Implementation
- Storage of Capacity Management data
- Demand management
- Modeling
- Application sizing
- Production of the capacity plan

Iterative Activities – are those activities that need to be carried out iteratively and form a natural cycle as illustrated in Figure 11-2. They operate within all the sub-processes of Capacity Management, and contribute to the capacity plan.

Storage of Capacity Management data – The information in the Capacity Management Database (CDB) forms the basis of performance and Capacity Management reporting as well as generation of capacity forecasts and capacity plans. The CDB contains business data, service data, technical data, financial data, and utilization data. Therefore, it is unlikely to be a single database or even a single type of data store. Like the CMDB, it should be thought of as a virtual collection and presentation of data from multiple stores.

Demand Management – is concerned with influencing demand for services or IT infrastructure due to physical and financial constraints over both the short and long terms. It operates within all three sub-processes. Demand management utilizes techniques such as differential charging or management directive to influence demand for services or infrastructure in an effort to either increase or reduce demand. This often happens in times of excess demand or partial failures of the infrastructure.

In periods of excess demand, charges for service may be increased to the point where demand matches capacity. This would be done to ensure critical services have capacity in situations where increasing capacity is too costly to justify. In periods of partial infrastructure failure, business critical services will be provided access to the infrastructure while all others will not. This ensures that the business receives maximum value for the infrastructure that remains functional.

The prime objective of Demand Management is to influence the demand for a computing resource and the use of that resource.

It is important to understand the difference between demand management and differential costing. Demand management is an activity in Capacity Management while differential costing is an accounting tool, discussed in Financial Management, which can be used to implement demand management.

Modeling – is concerned with making accurate predictions of future events as a result of a change. ITIL recognizes four types of modeling:

- Trend analysis
- Analytical modeling
- Simulation modeling
- Baseline modeling

The prime objective of modeling is to predict the behavior of IT services under a given volume and variety of work.

Application Sizing – is concerned with ensuring that applications are designed from the beginning, or during major upgrades to appropriately handle the capacity demands expected as documented in the capacity plan. An example of this would be designing a software application with an enterprise scale database based on two-year capacity projections when a departmental scale database would serve current demand. Although the up front cost will be increased, time and resources that otherwise would be spent on upgrading the software will be saved on the back end.

The primary objective of application sizing is to estimate the resource requirements to support a proposed application change or new application, to ensure that it meets its required service levels.

Production of the capacity plan – is concerned with producing a plan for capacity that takes into account business planning at all levels and documents in appropriate detail how IT will provide the required capacity over each planning period. This plan should be a living document that provides actionable information for day-to-day Capacity Management.

The capacity plan is a vital tool for IT budgeting. It should be published annually in time to be used in the budget process.

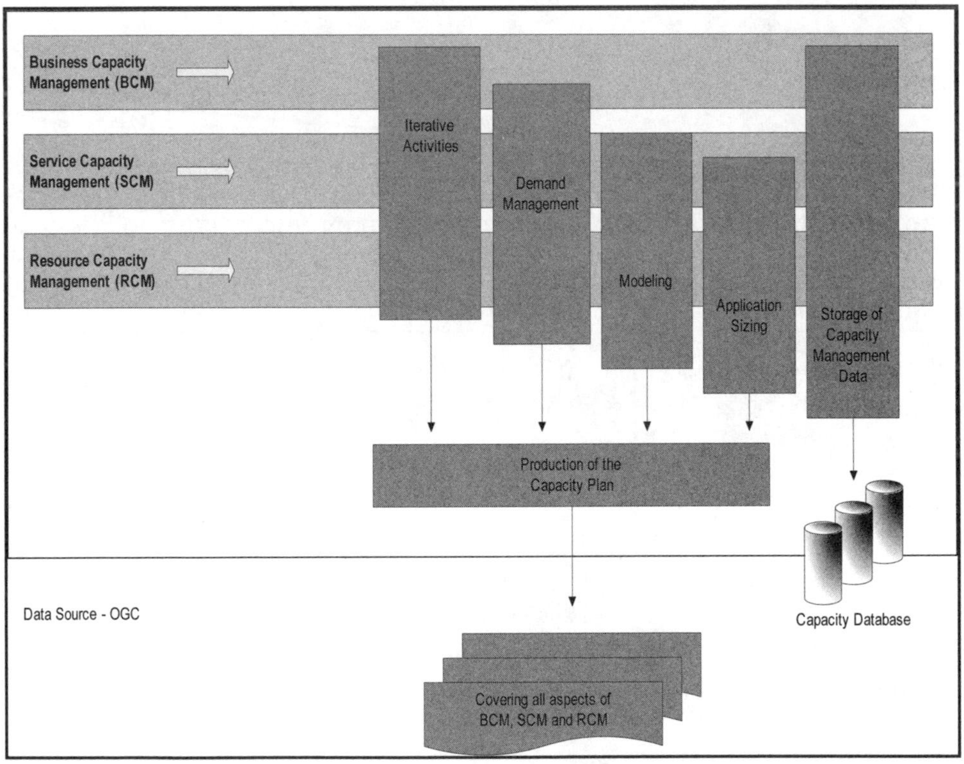

Figure 11-1: Activities in Capacity Management

The prime objective of capacity planning is to produce a plan that documents the current levels of resource utilization and service performance. After consideration of the business strategy and plans, it will forecast the future requirements for resources to support the IT services that underpin the business activities.

Iterative Activities

We are what we repeatedly do. Excellence, then, is not an act, but a habit.
– Aristotle

Figure 11-2 shows the ongoing or iterative activities of Capacity Management, and their relationship to one another.

The iterative process is identified by the solid arrows and includes:

- Monitoring.
- Analysis.
- Tuning.
- Implementation.

The iterative activities are supported by measurements, such as resource utilization thresholds and Service Level Management thresholds. The Capacity Management database supports the iterative activities and is a repository for their inputs and outputs. Some outputs of the iterative activities are Service Level Management exception reports and resource utilization exception reports.

Monitoring – is concerned with understanding what is going on in all aspects of the environment including components, services, and the business. It involves a wide range of techniques and technologies such as surveys and utilization counts to accomplish its goals.

Components are measured with internal and external tools that monitor items, such as CPU and memory utilization. Services require more complex monitoring tools that are capable of demonstrating the characteristics of the entire end-to-end service from the end-user's perspective. The business is monitored through management interactions; relationships; and soft measures, such as surveys.

Analysis – is concerned with understanding the implications of the data collected in the monitoring activities. Tools such as base-lining and "exception reporting" can be used to identify areas ripe for improvement or for increased monitoring over time.

Tuning – is concerned with acting on the collected and analyzed data to eliminate bottlenecks that limit capacity and performance. This is an activity that is coordinated with proactive problem management.

Implementation – is concerned with releasing those changes that have been identified in the monitoring, analysis, and tuning activities into the production environment. In cooperation with Problem Management, requests for change are created and changes are implemented through the managed change process.

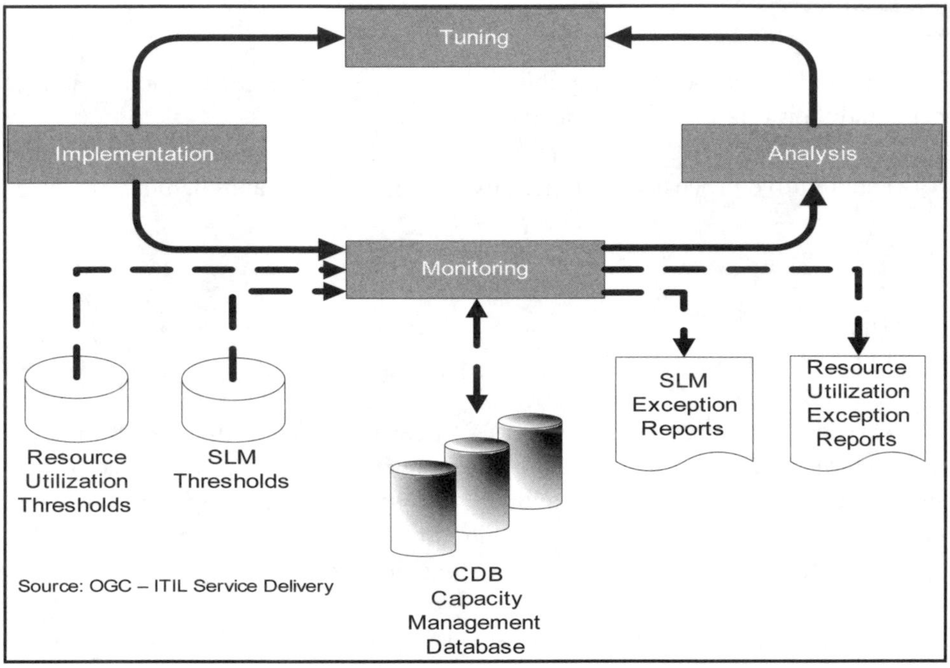

Figure 11-2: Iterative activities of Capacity Management

Proactive Activities

One of the tests of leadership is the ability to recognize a problem before it becomes an emergency.
– Arnold H. Glasow

Although Capacity Management works closely with Problem Management to react quickly to any disruptions in capacity, its primary role is to be proactive and ensure that acceptable capacity is available in every contingency and within acceptable budget constraints. This involves planning and developing infrastructure in advance of business changes.

Much of the unnecessary cost associated with IT comes from reacting to events in emergency mode as a result of poor planning and communication. It is Capacity Management's responsibility in coordination with Problem Management to ensure that proactive measures are taken wherever possible to eliminate the occurrence of emergency capacity events.

Some of the specific proactive activities are:

- Pre-empt performance problems.
- Produce utilization trend reports.
- Model potential changes to quantify effects and requirements.
- Ensure upgrades are deployed as they are needed, thus ensuring cost remain low while achieving capacity targets.
- Employ methods to actively and continuously improve capacity capabilities while reducing costs.

Capacity Planning

Let our advance worrying become advance thinking and planning.
– Sir Winston Churchill

The most central activity in Capacity Management is planning. Planning with the business to have IT services in place to meet changing business priorities, planning with IT to ensure that IT managers know what will be required of IT, and planning infrastructure improvements are all the responsibilities of Capacity Planning. Capacity Management maintains a "living document" that is called a capacity plan, which shows the current and expected levels of capacity into the future with an appropriate level of detail to identify how goals will be accomplished.

The capacity plan is essentially an investment plan and therefore should be published in time for budget planning every year. Updates should be published as capacity requirements change, or as budgets change. Formal capacity planning allows IT to defer expenditures until they are needed, to match capacity to business need, and to reduce costs as planned buying replaces panic buying. It also reduces operational risk and provides valuable information for development planning.

Conclusion

Capacity Management is all about ensuring that IT plans for and manages the capacity requirements for IT services in direct collaboration with business planning. It has three major sub-processes: business capacity management, service capacity management, and resource capacity management. It has well-defined activities that provide input for the capacity plan. The capacity plan is a vital tool for budgeting and should be published in time for use in the budgeting process.

Exam Preparation Questions

1. What is the goal of Capacity Management?
2. At what levels of business planning is Capacity Management involved?
3. What are the three sub-processes of Capacity Management?
4. What are the differences between the three sub-processes?
5. What are the nine activities in Capacity Management?
6. What are the iterative activities in Capacity Management?
7. What is the CDB and what does it contain?
8. What four types of modeling does ITIL recognize?
9. What are five specific proactive activities in Capacity Management?
10. When should the capacity plan be published?
11. Be able to define the following in ITIL terms:
    1. Demand management
    2. Modeling
    3. Application sizing

12

Availability Management

Introduction

Nothing ever built arose to touch the skies unless someone dreamed that it should, believed that it could, and willed that it must.
– Alfred Lord Tennyson

ITIL Availability Management is all about ensuring IT services are provided to the business when they are needed and in the way they are needed. Availability requirements are defined in service level agreements. It is the responsibility of Availability Management to monitor availability from an end-to-end perspective as detailed in the service level agreement. Availability Management also works with Problem Management to resolve issues on both a reactive and a proactive basis.

Goal of Availability Management

The goal of availability management is to optimize the capability of the IT infrastructure and supporting organization to deliver a cost effective and sustained level of availability that enables the business to satisfy its objectives.

Availability Management is essential for obtaining a high degree of customer and end-user satisfaction. Customers and end-users have different expectations and concerns regarding availability of services that require individualized focus in reporting. Perception of system availability and reliability is often more important to satisfaction than the reality. Therefore, Availability Management should make every effort to manage perception in action and in reporting.

Typically, very little effort is put into what availability really is and how it should be measured. When asked 'what level of availability is required', many IT managers respond by vaguely citing arbitrary statistics (three nines (99.9%) or five nines (99.999%)) assuming that all questions are answered by that response. In reality, this approach does not even begin to answer the questions that need to be answered to have effective Availability Management. Some of the initial questions that need to be asked about availability are:

- How should availability be defined in practical terms?
- How should unavailability be defined? For instance, if there are 100 users of a service and one of the users cannot access the service, is the service available? To what level is it available?
- What availability metrics should be captured?
- How should availability metrics be reported to the customer? To the end-user? To IT?

Guiding Principles of Availability

The secret of success is constancy of purpose.
– Benjamin Disraeli

The following three points are critical for understanding the value of an availability process and for providing direction towards improving availability:

1. Customers and end-users need the IT services that they depend upon to be available when they are needed. When these services are not available consistently as needed, it is very difficult for IT to maintain customers and end-user satisfaction resulting in a decline in the overall perception of IT.

2. In an environment where availability is the norm, one-time disruptions to service availability are excellent opportunities for IT to shine in its customer's and end-user's eyes. The manner in which IT responds to these incidents will be noted. IT will be viewed by the great majority as an organization of disciplined professionals if response is quick and effective; if communications are frequent, clear, and helpful; and if IT demonstrates how IT processes will be improved to ensure that the incident is an exception that will not be repeated.

3. Availability is critical to the business and is measured in business terms. For this reason, improvements in availability must be important and visible to the business in order to be perceived as valuable.

Terminology

If you wish to converse with me, define your terms
— Voltaire

In defining service level targets for availability, it becomes vital to have clearly-defined terms for typically provided levels of availability. Providing clear and unambiguous terminology and using it consistently provides for better customer and end-user relationships since misunderstandings leading to relationship issues are reduced.

Availability and *reliability* in non-ITIL organizations are often used interchangeably. In ITIL organizations, however, each has a specific meaning. Availability deals with accumulated downtime over a given period, while reliability deals with the frequency of downtime. In simple terms, a service can go down many times, but if restored very quickly could maintain an agreed level of availability. This occurs because the metric 'availability' only measures the accumulation of downtime. On the other hand, reliability measures how often a service goes down. Often it requires evaluating both metrics to gain a clear understanding of the overall availability picture and to determine appropriate corrective actions.

There are three levels of availability, identified by ITIL:

1. **High Availability** – attempts to shield end-users from the effects of component failures. Typical technical implementations include clustered fail-over configurations and redundant routing logic that allows routers to find alternate data paths when one link goes down.

2. **Continuous Operation** – attempts to shield end-users from the effects of planned downtime. Typical technical implementations include load-balancing or clustered configurations that allow for taking individual components off-line without disrupting the service as a whole.

3. **Continuous Availability** – attempts to shield end-users from the effects of planned and unplanned downtime. Typical technical implementations include load-balancing or clustered configurations that allow for both taking individual components off-line without disrupting service and for individual components to fail without impacting the service. It is a combination of high availability and continuous operation.

Unavailability is the key indicator of service quality perceived by the business and end-user. End-users and customers take availability for granted until it stops, then they become very focused on it. For end-users and customers, it is periods of unavailability and IT's reaction to unavailability that determines the perception of IT as a service provider.

Availability is underpinned by the *reliability* and *maintainability* of the IT infrastructure and by the effectiveness of the IT support organization. Following are the critical elements of availability:

- Availability of components
- Resilience to failure
- Quality of maintenance and support
- Quality, pattern, and extent of deployment of operational processes and procedures
- Security, integrity, and availability of data

Reliability is determined by:

1. *Reliability* of each component in the infrastructure delivering the service

2. *Level of resilience* designed and built into the infrastructure, or the ability of a component to fail and have that failure not impact service availability

Maintainability is another critical component of overall availability. It deals with how well the organization maintains services in an operational state and on how rapidly services are restored when they do fail. Even in the best run environments, IT services can fail. The occurrence of service failure introduces one overriding concern: the speed with which IT can return the service to an operational state. Given that with enough time every service will fail, IT should invest an appropriate amount of effort to ensure that services can be restored rapidly. Maintainability can be divided into seven separate stages around which maintainability improvements can be targeted:

1. Anticipation of failures
2. Detection of failures
3. Diagnosis of failures
4. Resolution of failures
5. Recovery from failures
6. Restoration of the data and IT service
7. Level of preventative maintenance applied

Serviceability is identical to *maintainability* in almost every way, with one significant difference: the responsible party is different and that changes the level of due diligence to be applied. *Serviceability* implies that there is a third party involved and that a contract exists to ensure performance. In other words, *maintainability* is internal to the company and *serviceability* is support provided by vendors.

Availability Management is the one process area other than Security Management that directly addresses *security.* Availability Management is concerned with security in terms of *confidentiality, integrity,* and *availability.* These terms are often referred to by the acronym CIA.

Vital Business Function (VBF) is a term that is used to reflect the business critical elements of a business process. In an ATM Banking scenario, dispensing cash is considered a VBF because it is the primary driver of customer satisfaction with the ATM service. It is a VBF because customers typically seek cash for very specific purchases that are immediately important to them. When the ATM fails to dispense cash, it often means that the customer cannot fulfill that purchase and will leave feeling deprived by the bank. In contrast, printing a statement would not be a VBF since printing a statement is seldom time sensitive, most customers would not be significantly upset if the latter function failed.

The Availability Process

A man who wants to do something will find a way; a man who doesn't will find an excuse.
– Stephen Dolley, Jr.

The major inputs of the availability process are divided into business and operational inputs. The inputs are:

Business Inputs:

- Business availability requirements
- Business impact assessment
- Availability, reliability, and maintainability requirements

Operational Inputs:

- Incident and problem data
- Configuration and monitoring data
- Service level achievements

The outputs are:

- Availability and recovery design criteria.
- IT infrastructure resilience and risk assessment.
- Agreed upon targets for availability, reliability, and maintainability.
- Reports of availability, reliability, and maintainability achieved.
- Availability monitoring.
- Availability improvement plans.

Measuring

To measure is to know. If you cannot measure it, you can not improve it.
– Lord Kelvin

Now that availability is given a precise definition, the question becomes how to measure availability as defined? This question can be refined a little by stating that technical issues are not a major concern here. Any good technical architect can design a technical measuring system that meets the measurement criteria. The concerns here are the management questions of what the technical measurement criteria are going to be and how those measurements help IT meet customer requirements. In order to set appropriate measurement criteria, one important question must be answered: What value is expected to be gained from measuring availability? It quickly becomes apparent that there are three primary groups who seek to measure value from availability metrics, each coming from three different perspectives: the customer perspective, the end-user perspective, and the IT perspective.

Providing appropriate metrics for these three groups requires designing a monitoring architecture that provides for both common metrics for all three groups and for individualized metrics for each group. In addition to a structure of metrics, there is a need for individualized reporting structures for each group. Each group speaks a slightly different language and has differing concerns regarding the information. Therefore, IT management must, if it desires to positively influence perceptions, design reporting structures that address the individualized needs of each group.

IT organizations that seek to actively manage perceptions will design a monitoring architecture that considers more than just technical measures. Sometimes technical measures do not provide enough information for customers and IT managers to make the best decisions. Think of measuring things such as perceptions, satisfaction, and expectations. Think about how to better understand end-users and customers in order to provide them with ever increasing value from measurement services. Look at monitoring as an opportunity to identify barriers to creating value that are both directly related to technology and related to the end-user experience when using technology.

Think about the experience of each of the three groups and about how IT can help each of these groups to contribute more value to the business. Some questions to ask are:

- Do end-users exhibit frustration with a particular part of a business process that could easily be improved with technology?
- Are end-users required to make multiple mouse clicks or key strokes for simple and common activities?
- Are customers unable to demonstrate the value of their business efforts due to missing metrics or poorly organized data?
- Does IT know what each customer's three highest business priorities are?
- What has IT done to help them achieve success on those priorities, lately?
- Does IT have a monitoring system that makes it efficient for IT staff to complete their jobs?
- Is IT staff inundated with pages due to non-emergency alerts after normal business hours? Is the impact on performance measured?
- Do critical systems often crash without warning, requiring unplanned after hours work?
- Do critical systems go unmonitored, because the organization does not realize they are critical?

What to Measure? IT Availability Metrics Model (ITAMM)

When you can measure what you are speaking about, and express it in numbers, you know something about it. But when you cannot measure it, when you cannot express it in numbers, your knowledge is of a meager and unsatisfactory kind.
– Lord Kelvin

The IT Availability Metrics Model or ITAMM can be used as a reminder that measurement of availability, reliability, maintainability, and response times for the following areas is critical:

- Vital business functions
- Application
- Data
- Network
- Key components

- Platform

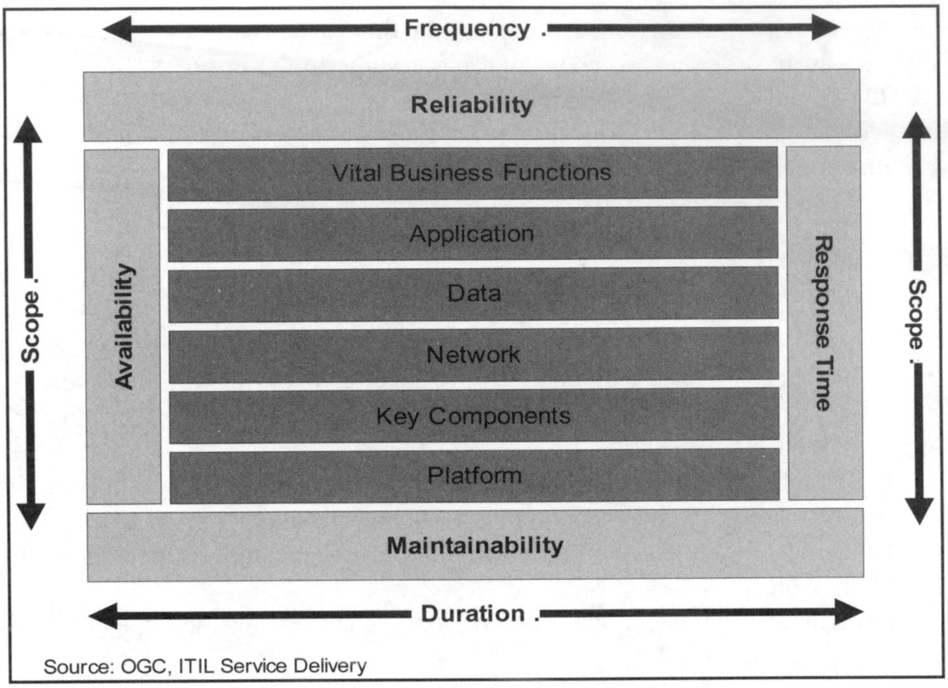

Figure 12-1: IT availability metrics model (ITAMM)

These elements should all be measured as part of an end-to-end service.

The IT availability metrics model (ITAMM) is a diagram that helps visualize the key components of availability measurement. Across the top of the ITAMM diagram, Figure 12-1, is reliability, which is concerned with how often service is disrupted or the frequency of disruption. Along the bottom is maintainability, which impacts how long each outage is sustained. To report on reliability, record how often the service is disrupted. To report on maintainability, record how long each outage lasted.

Along the outsides are availability and response time. Availability should be a measure of the actual availability against SLA targets. Response time should be measured to show the level of service commitment and as an indicator of end-user perception of IT. Inside the diagram are the key elements to measure.

When setting up monitoring architecture, this model can be used as a quick reference to ensure that each aspect of the architecture supplies the key measures on each of the key elements.

Reporting

Report me and my cause aright.
– William Shakespeare

IT generally reports availability information in a manner that makes sense for IT and that supports IT focused activities. This often leaves the business without a clear understanding of the availability situation. As a result, business leaders make decisions that might have been made differently given a clearer understanding. For instance, IT reports on technology components in technical terms, but rarely reports the impacts to business services. It is increasingly important therefore, if the perception of IT is to be improved, that IT learns to communicate effectively to the different groups that rely on IT reports for critical information.

There are three primary groups with which IT must communicate: end-users, customers, and internal IT groups. Typically, IT organizations design their communications to reach only one audience—themselves. Often, even that reporting is inadequate to the purpose. Communication is a crucial aspect of IT performance. If the perception of IT is to improve, then the communication skills of the IT organization must improve.

Communication is only effective if we speak the language of the recipient. Imagine traveling to another country and insisting that everyone there speak your language. We would consider that example illogical, recognizing that if someone does not speak or understand our language, we could not communicate effectively. The same is true within organizations; each professional group speaks its own language. They may speak English, but their professional terminology differs and their styles of communication differ. A major complicating factor is that differing professional groups will use the exact same term, but will each have a very precise but different definition for the term.

IT is unique in that it provides services to all departments and must interface effectively with each of them independently. In other words, IT needs to have a cooperative working relationship with each department and minimize conflict with each of them. In order for IT to effectively communicate among all groups or departments, it must be multilingual. IT must understand and be fluent in each group's terminology and communication styles. Communication between groups can elicit either cooperation or conflict; therefore, it is important that we utilize communication strategies that will promote cooperation.

Intentionally or inadvertently forcing business people to speak in IT language creates a coercive atmosphere that promotes hostility and negative perceptions, the very things that are detrimental to the wel-

fare of IT. Let's look at it from a personal perspective. If you feel pressured to do something you don't want to do, it is unlikely that you will do it (depending on your personality), and you will probably not have warm fuzzy feelings for the person who pressured you.

From an interpersonal perspective, the viable responses to feeling coerced are to: (1) refuse and be uncooperative, (2) counterattack and force a position, or (3) comply. Most people will fall in the first two categories, which causes conflict between the communicating parties. People in all three groups will probably have some level of negative feelings and perceptions towards the person who coerced them. When negative feelings or perceptions exist between two parties, conflict is high and cooperation is low. This is a bad place to be if you are trying to cooperatively meet business goals.

When IT forces customers and end-users to communicate in IT language, there are only 3 options and a 33% chance of compliance, which leaves most customers and end-users with a negative perception of IT. Conversely, speaking in the language of the recipient greatly increases the probability of cooperative, satisfied customers and end-users, which results in a more positive perception of IT.

– Christine Belaire, Ph.D.

End-users have three primary concerns regarding outages:

1. Frequency of impact –i.e. how often service is disrupted
2. Duration of impact – i.e. how long service is disrupted
3. Scope of impact - i.e. how many users were impacted

IT can take two primary approaches to report this information:

1. Impact by user minutes lost
2. Impact by business transaction

Another concern for end-users and a primary driver of end-user perceptions is response time for incidents. Often the primary factor in end-user perception of IT is how quickly and effectively IT responds when an incident is reported. Downtime can often be well tolerated if response times are seen to be rapid and information of concern is communicated appropriately.

Internal IT reporting should be focused on how IT component availability, reliability, and maintainability impact service availability. It should show areas that are functioning well in addition to the areas that are functioning poorly. It should highlight trends and give staff the ability to measure performance in an objective manner. With respect to availability, IT is primarily concerned with:

- The component view.
- Technical details.

- Exceptions.

The business is focused on availability in terms of:

- Vital business functions.
- Services.
- Data.
- Impact on the business.

As a result, IT should focus its message to the business on the following:

- Successes.
- Major milestones.
- Business concerns.
- Process based solutions.
- Professional responses.

When designing reports for the business, it is important to note the different approaches to information sharing and troubleshooting between business managers and IT managers. IT managers focus on technical details and exceptions. They see the world primarily from a black and white or break/fix perspective. Business managers on the other hand focus on business processes and improving outputs. They see the world from a 'shades of gray' or a tuning perspective. Failing to adjust communications to this reality is a primary reason for IT being perceived as negative and focused on problems instead of making things work.

Some questions to consider when designing a reporting process:

- How does IT reassure the business that availability issues are being improved in a professional, well-managed way?
- Can IT demonstrate that it is doing everything possible in a disciplined and structured manner to improve availability from both the customer's and end-user's perspective?
- Which methods will IT employ to ensure that communications are appropriate?

Availability Improvement

Always dream and shoot higher than you know how to. Don't bother just to be better than your contemporaries or predecessors. Try to be better than yourself.
– William Faulkner

Following are some of the primary tools (methods) that Availability Management utilizes to improve availability performance:

Component Failure Impact Analysis (CFIA)

CFIA output provides valuable information for designing new IT Services and for upgrading IT services. It identifies the impact that will be produced by failure of any given component in a service. It does this by providing:

- Single points of failure that can impact IT availability.
- The impact of component failure on the business operation and end-users.
- Component and people dependencies.
- Component recovery timings.
- The need to identify and document recovery options.
- The need to identify and implement risk reduction measures.

CFIA also helps Availability Management and IT Service Continuity Management determine either where high availability risk reduction measures, or where redundancy is needed.

Fault Tree Analysis (FTA)

Fault Tree Analysis (FTA) is a technique that is used to determine the chain of events that can cause a disruption of IT services. This technique, in conjunction with calculation methods, can offer detailed models of availability.

The main advantages of FTA are:

- It can be used for availability calculations.
- Operations can be performed on the resulting fault tree that correspond with design options.
- The desired level of detail in the analysis can be chosen.

FTA makes a representation of a chain of events, using Boolean notation. Essentially, FTA distinguishes the following events:

- **Basic events** — Terminal points for the fault tree, e.g. power failure, operator error. Basic events are not investigated in greater depth. If basic events are investigated in further depth, they automatically become resulting events.
- **Resulting events** —Intermediate nodes in the fault tree resulting from a combination of events. The top most point in the fault tree is usually a failure of the IT Service.
- **Conditional events** — Events that only occur under certain conditions, e.g. failure of the air-conditioning equipment only affects the IT service if equipment temperature exceeds the serviceable values.
- **Trigger events** — Events that trigger other events, e.g. power failure detection equipment can trigger automatic shutdown of IT Services.

These events can be combined using logic operators:

- **AND-gate** — The resulting event only occurs when all input events occur simultaneously.
- **OR-gate** — The resulting event occurs when one or more of the input events occurs.
- **Exclusive OR-gate** — The resulting event occurs when one and only one of the input events occurs.
- **Inhibit gate** — The resulting event only occurs when the input condition is not met.

CRAMM

CRAMM stands for CCTA Risk Analysis and Management Method. This is the preferred risk management methodology for the British government. It involves the activities of risk analysis and risk management.

Risk Analysis - involves the identification and assessment of the level of risks.

Risk Management - involves the identification, selection, and adoption of countermeasures, and the reduction of risks to an acceptable level.

This approach, when applied via a formal method ensures that coverage is complete, together with sufficient confidence that:

- All possible risks and countermeasures have been identified.
- All vulnerabilities have been identified and their levels accurately assessed.
- All threats have been identified and their levels accurately assessed.
- All results are consistent across the broad spectrum of the IT infrastructure reviewed.
- All expenditure on selected countermeasures can be justified.

Calculating Availability

There are three methods identified in ITIL for calculating availability. The first is the basic availability calculation, the second is a more involved calculation that takes into account multiple end-users, and the third shows how to measure availability of a service chain.

Exercises:

Basic Availability calculation

Basic Availability

$$\left(Availability\% = \frac{(AST - DT)}{(AST)} \times 100\right)$$

AST = Agreed upon service time
DT = Actual downtime during agreed upon service time

Example:

A 24x7 IT service requires a weekly two-hour planned downtime period for application maintenance. Following the completion of the weekly maintenance an application software error occurs, which results in three hours of unplanned downtime.

What is the level of availability?

Answers: See Appendix A

End-User Perspective calculation

End-User Availability

$$\left(EUA\% = \frac{EUPT - EUDT}{EUPT} \times 100\right)$$

EUPT = End-User Processing Time = AST x Total number of users
EUDT[1] = End-User Down Time = DT x Total number of users impacted
EUDT is shown per incident.
EUA requires Total EUDT = $\Sigma(EUDT)$ per unit

Example:

Consider a 24-hour x 7-day service having 1,000 users and a two hour planned downtime slot per week.

Given the CFIA information in Figure 12-2 what is the EUA?

Incident #	Date	Time	Duration (mins)	Incident Description	Failed Component	User Impact	EUDT (mins)
1	1 Oct	09:25	60	Payments Database full	Payments Database	50	3,000
2	4 Oct	12:48	25	Server hang - rebooted	Server XYZ	20	500
3	5 Oct	09:56	125	Host operating system failure	Host	1000	125,000
4	5 Oct	16:40	20	Fuse blown in power supply	Workstation A	1	20
			230				128,520

Figure 12-2: CFIA documentation

Answers: See Appendix A

Total Infrastructure Availability Calculation

Serial Configuration

$$ServiceAvailability\% = (Comp1 \times Comp2 \times Comp3 \times Comp4 \times 100)$$

Component #1 = Host = 98%
Component #2 = Network = 98%
Component #3 = Server = 97.5%
Component #4 = Workstation = 96%

What is the total availability of this series from the end-user perspective?

The series calculation provides an example of availability from the end-user perspective. Think of this in terms of silos and services. Each IT silo may individually have seemingly respectable availability numbers which mask the fact that end-to-end service availability is poor.

An important aspect to serial availability calculations is that the more components in series the faster the service availability declines. One implication of this is that for services with many serial components very high levels of silo availability may be required to deliver service levels expected by the business.

Answers: See Appendix A

Service Outage Analysis (SOA)

SOA is a structured approach to identify end-to-end availability improvement opportunities that deliver benefits to the user. Many of the activities are closely aligned with Problem Management.

The high-level objectives of SOA are to:

- Identify the underlying causes of service interruption to the end-user.
- Assess the effectiveness of the IT support organization and key processes.
- Produce reports detailing major findings and recommendations.
- Initiate a program of activities to implement the agreed upon recommendations.
- Measure improvements derived from SOA driven activities.

In short, SOA is a highly structured and specialized project which has been designed to root out availability issues.

The Expanded Incident Life Cycle

The Expanded Incident Life Cycle is a tool that shows critical measurements required from Incident Management and Problem Management to pinpoint areas that offer the greatest opportunity for improving availability.

The following are the measurement points identified by the Expanded Incident Life Cycle:

- **Occurrence of the incident** – The time at which the user becomes aware of the fault, or when the fault is identified by other means.
- **Detection** – The service provider is informed of the fault. The incident status is now 'reported.'
- **Response** – The time it takes the process to respond to the registered incident.
- **Repair** – The time it takes to resolve the fault.
- **Service Recovery** – The time it takes to restore service. This includes configuration, initialization, and notifying the end-user.

Following are some of the questions to ask when seeking to minimize detection time:

- Do all end-users know how to reach the Service Desk?
- Is it easy to do so?
- Are the phone prompts difficult or cumbersome?
- What is the wait time?
- Are end-users reluctant to call SD for any reason?
- Are there unmanaged super-users trying to resolve the problem first?

Following are some of the questions to ask when seeking to minimize response times:

- How quick and efficient is the escalation process?
- How consistent is it?
- How long does it take to find the correct resource?

Following are some of the questions to ask when seeking to minimize repair times:

- Does IT have the proper problem resolution tools readily available?
- Are expert technical staff assigned on-call status for urgent reactive incidents?
- Do rapid response teams exist?
- Do they practice?
- Are they cross-discipline teams?

Following are some of the questions to ask, when seeking to minimize recovery times:

- Does configuration baseline information exist and can it be found?
- Are data backup processes and restore processes functioning efficiently and quickly?
- Are startup dependencies documented and available?
- Are there potential undetected problems, caused by this outage?

All of these measurement times are potential areas where overall downtime can be reduced. Knowing specifically where time is being lost in the process is critical to reducing overall downtime. Does your Service Desk organization accurately and reliably collect information at this level of detail?

Some common reporting data and performance metrics that come from this information are:

- **Mean time to repair (MTTR)** – average downtime
- **Mean time between failures (MTBF)** – average uptime
- **Mean time between system incidents (MTBSI)** – mean time between the occurrences of two consecutive incidents

$$MTBSI = MTTR + MTBF$$

Conclusion

Availability Management is concerned with ensuring that IT services are provided to the business when they are needed and how they are needed. It accomplishes this by clearly defining what availability means in terms of end-user and customer satisfaction and by designing a monitoring architecture that collects appropriate metrics and produces appropriate reports for each of the three data consumers: end-users, customers, and IT itself. It accomplishes the first two by learning to speak business language and to focus efforts around end-user facing services. It also works closely with Problem Management, applying proven availability tools to reactively and proactively resolve current and potential problems with availability.

Exam Preparation Questions

1. What is the goal of Availability Management?
2. What are the three principles of availability?
3. What are the three levels of availability defined by ITIL?
4. How do reliability and availability differ?
5. What are the seven stages of maintainability?
6. Availability Management is concerned with security in relation to ________, _________ and ________.
7. How do maintainability and serviceability differ?
8. List four inputs and four outputs of the Availability Management process.
9. What three groups are consumers of availability measurement services?
10. What are the three primary concerns end-users have about service outages?
11. What are the two approaches for reporting service outages to end-users?
12. Internal IT reporting should be focused on how IT component _____________, ___________, and _______________ impact service availability.
13. The business is focused on availability in terms of ___________, ____________, ____________, and ________________ .
14. What are the eight methods introduced by ITIL for improving availability?
15. What is the formula for calculating basic availability?
16. What is the formula for calculating availability from an end-user perspective?
17. What is the formula for calculating total infrastructure availability?
18. Be able to define the following in ITIL terms:
    1. Availability

2. High availability
3. Continuous operation
4. Continuous availability
5. Un-availability
6. Reliability
7. Maintainability
8. Serviceability
9. VBF
10. SPOF
11. ITAMM
12. MTTR
13. MTBF
14. MTBSI

13

IT Service Continuity Management

Introduction

There is no such thing as "zero risk."
– William Driver

IT Service Continuity Management is responsible for ensuring that all business continuity measures implemented by the business are fully supported by IT. This involves setting up an IT Service Continuity structure that supports all of the business continuity needs. As is normal with ITIL, this chapter does not address technical details but management approaches, techniques, and terminology that provide a framework within which the technical aspects of continuity management can be implemented. The entire focus is on providing for recovery from disastrous events in direct support of the business continuity plan.

Much of this chapter deals with planning. Disastrous events, thankfully, do not happen every day. Disaster planning, however, is an ongoing event. Just as fire fighters plan and train regularly in order to effectively respond to fires, so too must IT Service Capacity Management teams plan and train to effectively respond to major business disruptions.

ITIL breaks down the implementation and ongoing activities of IT Service Continuity Management into four stages. Each of these stages contains specific activities to be performed.

It differs from Availability Management in that it is responsible for large scale loss of services due to a disastrous event. Availability Management is responsible for the day-to-day provision of service availability.

Goal of IT Service Continuity Management

The goal of IT Service Continuity Management is to support the overall business continuity management process by ensuring that the required IT technical and service facilities can be recovered within required and agreed upon business time-scales.

In order to support business continuity, IT must take responsibility for all of its activities:

- Assess the risks to IT service continuity and the impact that any disruption to service may have on the business.
- Identify critical business services and ensure that preventative measures are applied based on potential risks and severity of impact.
- Determine a work breakdown structure that ensures that services are restored within the time frames required by the business.
- Manage risk by implementing mitigation and contingency plans.
- Define the desired approach to restore service.
- Develop and test recovery plans and maintain a master recovery plan.

ITIL addresses continuity management as a comprehensive approach to ensure that the business can recover from disaster. For that reason, ITIL identifies two specific aspects to continuity management:

Business Continuity Management (BCM) – is responsible for planning business recovery from disaster. It creates and implements the master recovery plan that the entire business follows. Each organization within the business may have requirements for specific recovery planning that is unique to it. For instance manufacturing will have specific responsibility for reconstituting production lines. In this manner, IT has responsibility for reconstituting IT services.

IT Service Continuity Management (ITSCM) – is responsible for restoring IT services in response to disasters in support of the business continuity management master plan. Figure 13-1 shows all of the activities in IT Service Continuity

Management organized by stages. The stages are sequential and serve to highlight the dependencies between activities and groups of activities.

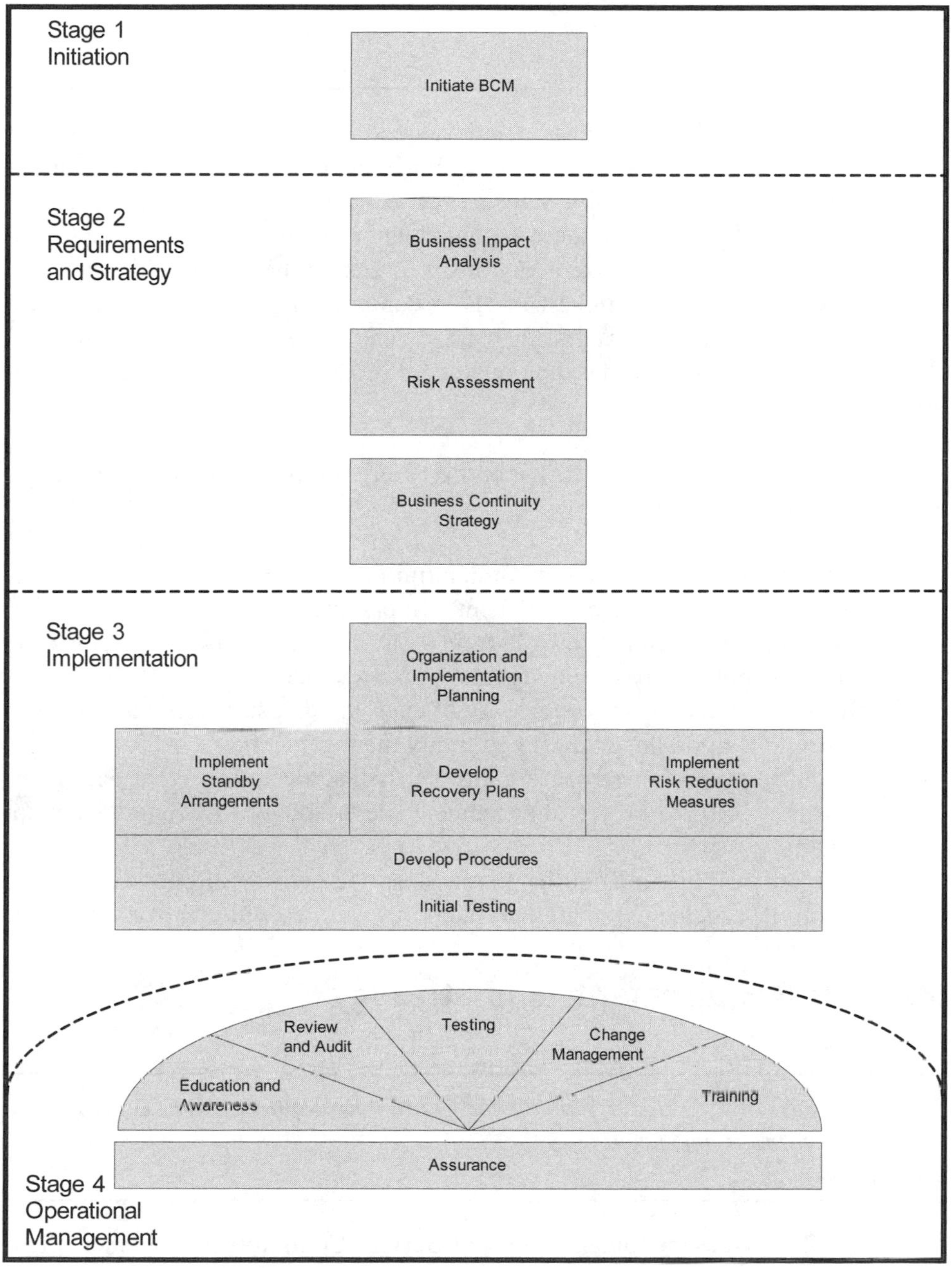

Figure 13-1: IT Service Continuity process model

Stage 1: Initiation

The most important key to achieving great success is to decide upon your goal and launch, get started, take action, move.
– John Wooden

IT Service Continuity Management is dependent on how well the business as a whole implements business continuity management. There is a natural limit to how much IT Service Continuity Management can accomplish in an environment where little or no business continuity management is conducted. IT Service Continuity Management should make every effort to ensure that its activities are supported and budgeted at the highest levels in conjunction with an active business continuity effort. Initiating continuity management is often a major organizational change and requires significant diplomatic skill, executive buy-in, and organizational agility.

The initiation process affects the entire IT organization and is where the following activities are conducted:

- **Policy setting** — is the activity of determining the boundaries or parameters within which continuity management will operate.
- **Specify terms of reference and scope** — is the activity of defining roles and areas of responsibility within continuity management
- **Allocate resources** — is the activity of ensuring that sufficient resources are in place to support the goals of continuity management.
- **Define the project organization and control structure** — is the activity of applying structured project management methodologies to continuity management.
- **Agree on project and quality plans** — is the activity of obtaining buy-in and active participation of all individuals and groups within the organization.

Stage 2: Requirements and Strategy

Every business must always plan ahead, either to capitalize on success or to reverse the trend if not successful.
– Anonymous

Stage 2 provides the foundation for IT Service Continuity Management. This is an important part of the process because structures typically survive disasters only if their foundations are well constructed. Of all the components that are critical to a structure's survival, none is more important in more situations than its foundation. Organizations are no different. Furthermore, the strength of the foundation significantly impacts the costs that will be incurred by the recovery effort.

Stage 2 can be effectively split into two sections:

1. **Requirements** – Perform business impact analysis and risk assessment.
2. **Strategy** – Determine and agree on risk reduction measures and recovery options to support the requirements.

Requirements:

Business Impact Analysis

The Business Impact Analysis (BIA) is an activity that identifies potential losses that a company is likely to endure if a disaster occurs. To do a BIA effectively, the organization must identify all of the critical business processes and their dependent sub-services (Service Catalog). For each of the business services assessments, the potential business impacts are recorded. This information is the basis for continuity management budgeting and recovery planning.

The business impact analysis also identifies:

- The form that the damage or loss may take including lost income, additional costs, damaged reputation, loss of goodwill, and loss of competitive advantage.
- How the degree of damage or loss is likely to escalate after a service disruption.
- The staffing, skills, facilities, and services (including the IT services) necessary to enable critical and essential business processes to continue operating at a minimum acceptable level.
- The time within which minimum levels of staffing, facilities, and services should be recovered.
- The time within which all required business processes and supporting staff, facilities, and services should be fully recovered.

Business services are ranked based on their importance to the business and the need to have them restored rapidly. Those with the greatest need are restored first, which requires first restoring the critical sub-services that support the business service.

Impacts are measured against particular scenarios for each business process, such as an inability to process transactions or to send invoices to customers and ensuring that cash flow is uninterrupted. They typically fall into one or more of the following categories:

- Failure to achieve agreed upon internal service levels
- Financial loss
- Additional costs
- Immediate and long-term loss of market share
- Breach of law, regulations, or standards
- Risk to personal safety
- Political, corporate, or personal embarrassment
- Breach of moral responsibility
- Loss of goodwill
- Loss of credibility
- Loss of image and reputation
- Loss of operational capability; for example, in a command and control environment

Risk Assessment – is the activity that determines the likelihood of any given disastrous event occurring and determining the level of service disruption that is likely to result. The science of risk assessment is supported by many risk analysis methodologies resulting from consistently applied statistical principles. CRAMM is the risk assessment methodology endorsed by ITIL and is the preferred methodology of the British government.

IT Service Continuity Strategy - when it comes to strategies for dealing with risk ITIL introduces two options:

1. Mitigation, i.e. risk reduction
2. Contingency, i.e. disaster recovery

Mitigation has to do with reducing the likelihood that an event will occur or that it will disrupt service if it does occur. Typical mitigation or risk reduction measures include:

- A backup and recovery strategy.
- Elimination of single points of failure, such as electrical power, access to facilities, etc.
- Outsourcing services to more than one supplier.
- Resilient IT systems.
- Improved security controls.

Contingency has to do with recovering from an event when it does happen. Contingency or recovery plans need to be prepared for:

- People and accommodation.
- IT systems and networks.

- Critical services, such as power, communications, water.
- Critical assets, such as paper records and reference materials.

There are six recovery options that an organization can choose from when implementing contingency plans:

1. **Do nothing** – In some cases the organization has determined that recovery is too expensive and that no recovery attempts will be made. This is a decision to be made at the highest organizational levels.
2. **Manual work-arounds** – In some cases a service can be provided manually. Although this is becoming more rare as automation increases, there are some cases where the organization may choose to simply revert to the manual method.
3. **Reciprocal arrangements** – These arrangements were typically seen in the mainframe era. Companies would make arrangements with other companies to provide access to computer equipment for some period if the other company experiences a disaster.
4. **Gradual recovery** – Is often called "Cold Standby." It allows for 72 hours or longer to recover services. It often provides a recovery site that is an empty shell with a minimum of basic services including cabling, air-conditioning, etc.
5. **Intermediate recovery** – Is often called "Warm Standby." It allows for between 24 and 72 hours for recovery. It requires a recovery site with all basic services and configured hardware.
6. **Immediate recovery** – Is often called "Hot Standby." It allows for recovery in 24 hours or less. It requires standby facilities that are in a high state of readiness, which may even be an exact replica of the production environment with all data and services kept in exactly the same state as the production environment in realtime.

Recovery facilities come in several variations that are a combination of four basic ideas:

Dedicated facilities – are those facilities that are reserved for use by one specific company and can either be owned by the company or leased from a third party.

Non-dedicated facilities – are those facilities that may be shared by two or more companies. They work on the principle that most disasters are localized. This principle allows a facilities provider to have a small number of facilities support a larger number of companies. In normal circumstances, only a few companies experience disasters at any one time, and adequate facilities exist to support their needs.

These types of facilities are excellent for localized disasters, but inadequate for large scale disasters affecting many companies. The primary reason these sites are utilized is that they cost less than dedicated sites.

Fixed facilities – are those facilities housed in buildings that cannot be moved.

Portable facilities – are those facilities housed in portable buildings or trailers that can be positioned in multiple locations depending on need.

The possible combinations are:

- Dedicated – fixed
- Non-dedicated – fixed
- Dedicated – portable
- Non-dedicated – portable

Students should be very familiar with the six recovery options and any associated timeframes. Students should also be familiar with the types and combinations of facilities.

Stage 3: Implementation

There is really no insurmountable barrier save your own inherent weakness of purpose.
– Ralph Waldo Emerson

The Implementation stage involves six activities:

1. Organization and implementation planning
2. Implementing standby arrangements
3. Developing recovery plans
4. Implementing risk-reduction measures
5. Developing procedures
6. Initial testing

Organization and Implementation Planning

Planning is a crucial step in IT service continuity management. If an organization is lucky; planning, testing, and practicing is all that it will ever do. However, for those organizations that do experience disasters, the planning, testing, and practicing will enable the business to recover quickly and may make the difference between survival and extinction.

There are three tiers of recovery effort that need to be identified in organizational planning:

1. Executive tier – which has overall authority and control for all recovery efforts.
2. Coordination tier – which is responsible for coordinating the overall effort within the organization.
3. Recovery tier – which includes the individuals and teams responsible for implementing the recovery plans.

There are three levels of planning that need to be considered overall:

1. Coordination planning
2. Key support function planning
3. Recovery team planning

Coordination planning includes the following formal plans:

- Emergency response plan
- Damage assessment plan
- Salvage plan
- Vital records plan
- Crisis management and public relations plan

Key support function planning includes the following formal plans:

- Accommodation and services plan
- Computer systems and network plan
- Telecommunication plan
- Security plan
- Personnel plan
- Finance and administration plan

Recovery team planning includes the following elements:

- Members
- Detailed task lists
- Support agreements

Implement Standby Arrangements

Recovery from disaster requires that standby arrangements exist and can be implemented. They include providing standby facilities and equipment as well as building standby infrastructure and managing contracts with third-party suppliers. These arrangements are the contingency options chosen in stage 2. In stage 3, plans for implementing these options are created.

Develop Recovery Plans

The recovery plans and the proof that they can be effectively executed are the deliverables of continuity management short of a disaster actually occurring. Therefore, developing the plans is the major activity of IT Service Continuity Management.

Implement Risk Reduction Measures

Typical risk reduction measures are:

- Provide for UPS capabilities
- Develop fault tolerant systems
- Offsite storage and archiving
- Duplication of data storage
- Spare equipment configured and ready

Develop Procedures

It may be necessary to have technical people, who are unfamiliar with the systems to restore the systems. For this reason, detailed procedures should be in place and available when needed.

Initial Testing

Testing is a critical part of the overall IT Service Continuity Management process and is the only way of ensuring that the selected strategy, standby arrangements, logistics, business recovery plans, and procedures will work in practice.

Stage 4: Operational Management

Lots of folks confuse bad management with destiny.
– Elbert Hubbard

IT environments are in a constant state of change, which causes continuity management plans to quickly become outdated. Resources need to be applied to ensure that the plans reflect the current state of the organization at all times. Therefore, continuity management needs to be a part of every change decision. Stage 4 includes the activities that keep the plans relevant and include:

- **Education and awareness** — Everyone needs to be aware that plans are in place, and they should know what their responsibilities are under the plans.
- **Review** — Things change constantly in the business and in IT. These changes need to be accurately reflected in the planning, which requires a consistent review process.
- **Testing** — Testing should be conducted on a regular basis to ensure that the process will work as needed, when needed.
- **Change control** — IT Service Continuity Management should be a required part of Change Management so that all changes are accurately reflected in IT Service Continuity Management planning and provisioning. In addition, IT Service Continuity Management needs should be reflected in all project plans, and funding should be identified.
- **Training** — Everyone involved in the recovery process should undergo appropriate planning to ensure that they can do what is required of them when it becomes necessary.
- **Assurance** – The final process in the IT Service Continuity Management lifeycle involves obtaining assurance that the quality of the IT Service Continuity Management deliverables is accceptable to senior business management and that the operational management processes are working satisfactorily.

Conclusion

IT Service Continuity Management is responsible for supporting business efforts to recover from disaster. It acts in concert with and takes its direction from business continuity management. Its activities are organized in a 4-stage framework that provides for a logical flow. It differs from Availability Management in that Continuity Management is responsible for large-scale loss of services due to a disastrous event, and Availability Management is responsible for the day-to-day provision of service availability.

Exam Preparation Questions

1. What is the goal of IT Service Continuity Management?
2. IT Service Continuity Management efforts are critically dependent on ________________.
3. What are the four stages of IT Service Continuity Management?
4. What are the activities in each stage of IT Service Continuity Management?
5. What are the six IT recovery options?
6. What is the time period allowed for a gradual recovery?
7. What is the time period allowed for an intermediate recovery?
8. What is the time period allowed for an immediate recovery?
9. What variations of recovery facilities are available?
10. What three tiers of recovery effort need to be identified in organizational planning?
11. What are the three levels of planning needed in IT Service Continuity Management?
12. What are the five types of plans in coordination planning?
13. What are the six types of plans in key support function planning?
14. What are the three types of plans in recovery team planning?
15. List five typical risk reduction measures for IT Service Continuity Management.

Part IV

SECURITY MANAGEMENT

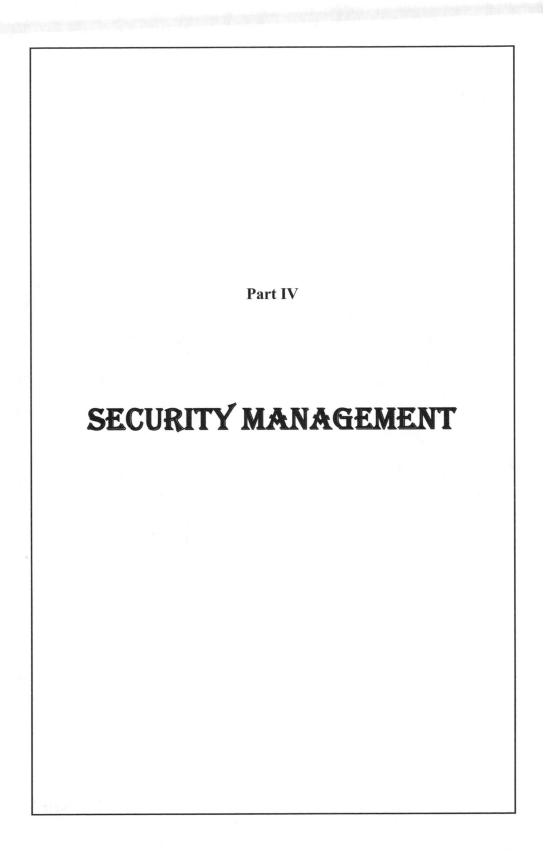

Introduction

Part IV covers the ITIL book *Best Practice for Security Management.*

Security Management is different from the other process areas in that it spans all three levels of management: strategic, tactical, and operational. As is the case in the other ITIL books, *ITIL Security Management* deals only with management best practice and not with technical solutions. This section lays out a structure for managing security that is holistic in nature. Security depends on all parts of the IT environment working together to ensure that all other parts remain secure. As the old saying goes "a chain is only as strong as its weakest link." Security is the same, the environment is only as secure as its weakest component. Therefore, the aim of Security Management is to ensure that all components of the IT environment are designed and implemented in a manner that keeps all the other components secure.

The service and process approaches are ideal for this type of security effort. Each approach serves to identify each of the components that make up either a service or process chain. Simply by documenting and visualizing each of the links in the chain, the activity of identifying weak links is greatly enhanced. As Dr. Deming often said about delivering quality, make problems visible so that they can be corrected. In security we need to make weakness visible so that they can be strengthened.

14

IT Security Management

Introduction

Never take anything for granted.
– Benjamin Disraeli

IT Security Management is the process of managing a defined level of security for information, IT services, and infrastructure. It is covered separately in its own ITIL book primarily because it is a special process area that interacts with every other process area at each of the levels; strategic, tactical, and operational.

It is IT Security Management's responsibility to enable and ensure that:

- Security controls exist and are accomplishing their objectives.
- Effective processes exist and that security incidents are given appropriate attention and management oversight.
- Audit processes exist and are implemented to ensure that results demonstrate the compliance of security controls against security policy.
- Reports are produced to show the status of information security.

Security policy is not the responsibility of IT Security Management. It's the responsibility of an organization's executive management. The job of IT security management is to ensure that IT security policy provides the level of security called for by the corporate security policy and to ensure that executive management has the required IT specific information needed to make informed policy decisions. A solid security management program needs to have complete support and funding from senior management. The Top-Down Approach is the type of model that should be followed when implementing a security management program.

An analogy of the separation of policy making and implementation between business and IT is the separation in the government where elected politicians make policy and the military carries out the policy. The concept was stated this way in the movie "Top Gun;" "We do not make policy, gentlemen. Civilians, elected officials do that. We are the instruments of that policy."

A solid, well-tuned IT Security Management process is like a fine-tuned athlete's body. The athlete requires proper nutrients, rest, exercise, mental alertness, strength, speed and endurance to be at optimal levels when competing. The same applies to a successful IT Security Management process. All the components (people, processes and technology) in IT Security Management must work together to achieve optimal levels of security. A breakdown in the athlete's regimen will cause a breakdown in her performance. A breakdown in any process, technology, or role component will cause a breakdown in the IT Security Management process affecting the overall confidentiality, integrity, and availability of critical assets and information.

Due Care and Due Diligence

Senior management is ultimately responsible for the protection of company assets and data. The information owner and senior management are responsible for protecting and classifying the data of the company and making sure only authorized personnel have access to the data. The owners of the data are expected to practice *due care*, which means that the owners will take the necessary steps to protect the assets and data of the company. Some examples of necessary steps to protect company assets and data include documented security policies, procedures, and standards, and implementing technical security systems. *Due diligence* is the act of understanding the current threats and risks, while *due care* is focused on implementing countermeasures to protect against unexpected events and identified threats.

Security Terms and Definitions

Many security terms are used interchangeably when in reality they are not the same thing. For example, the terms "risk," "threat," "vulnerability" and "exposure" are often used interchangeably, but in actuality they each have specific meanings. Below are clear descriptions for commonly used security terms.

- **Threat** - Potential danger to an asset. An example of a threat would be a computer worm or virus.

- **Threat agent** - The hacker taking advantage of a known vulnerability. For example, leaving your front door unlocked to your home would represent the vulnerability. The threat in this example would occur if an intruder took advantage of the current vulnerability, the unlocked door in order to break into your house and steal your valuables. The intruder in this example is the threat agent.
- **Risk** - Likelihood of the threat happening. It is the possibility and probability that a threat agent will exploit the current vulnerability. For example, if your web servers have ports wide open to the Internet without any firewall protection, you have a high probability that a hacker (i.e. threat agent) will take advantage of this vulnerability to compromise your web servers.
- **Exposure** - Situation of being exposed to potential losses from a threat. For example, if your system has been compromised by a hacker and then critical files have been deleted then you have already been exposed since loss has already occurred.
- **Vulnerability** - Weakness in system that threatens the confidentiality, availability, and integrity of an asset. A great example of this would be an unpatched server.
- **Countermeasure** - Control set in place to mitigate potential loss. Examples of this would include firewalls, strong password management, security guards, and intrusion detection systems.

There is a constant battle to keep a company's infrastructure and business well protected from computer and network attacks. It is of critical importance to have excellent people, processes, and technologies working together to thwart any potential attacks on the company's infrastructure, assets, or data.

The Business Perspective

If you think technology can solve your security problems, then you don't understand the problems and you don't understand the technology.
– Bruce Schneier

ITIL identifies two high level dimensions in which information is to be supplied and secured.

1. **Internal -** an organization can only function properly and make the best decisions if it has access to complete, accurate, and timely information.
2. **External -** an organization's success is dependent upon the quality of the information it has at its disposal. Based on this, it can introduce and supply products or services in the form that the market demands.

The following three concepts confidentiality, integrity, and availability are the foundation of information value.

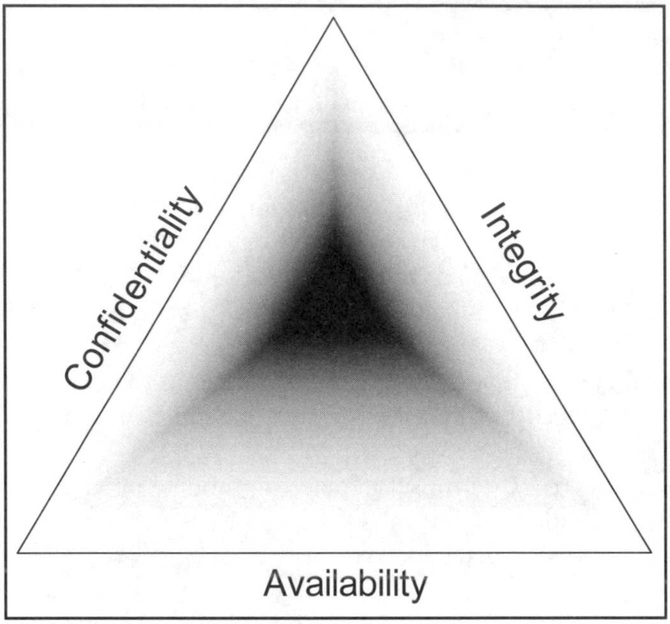

Figure 14-1: CIA

- **Confidentiality** – is preventing unauthorized disclosure of information. An example of a breach of confidentiality is if a criminal deceptively obtains information from the bank's security team to steal customer information that allows theft to take place. Confidentiality is also known as secrecy, sensitivity, and privacy.
- **Integrity** – is preventing unauthorized modification of information. An example of a breach of integrity is someone intercepting a message intended for another and modifying the message without either the sender or receiver knowing about it. Accuracy and completeness of information is the hallmark of integrity.
- **Availability** – is having usable information available for some purpose. An example of a breach of availability is if a disgruntled employee changes file settings that prohibit authorized users from gaining access to the information when needed.

Security Controls

Never underestimate the time, expense, and effort an opponent will expend to break a code.
– Robert Morris

If executive management is serious about effectively implementing security policies, those policies must come with appropriate allocation of resources.

There are four forms of security controls identified by ITIL:

- **Organizational** – controls provide clear roles, responsibilities, and reporting procedures that match the needs of the business and of IT. Separation of duties is critical to establish accountability for specific process controls. Organizational controls are concerned with what to do and how to report it.
- **Physical** – controls limit access to facilities. Examples include surveillance cameras, security guards, and intrusion detection systems. A sound recommendation is to provide a layered approach to physical security utilizing a combination of physical controls. An example of this is to include intrusion detection systems combined with surveillance cameras and physical security patrols. Physical controls can be thought of as anything that can be felt or touched.
- **Technical** – controls are utilized to augment the ability of individuals to implement organizational, physical, and procedural controls. They also serve to protect technical systems from technology based intrusions.
- **Procedural** – controls include policies, standards, procedures, and guidelines. An example of this would be Change, Release and Configuration Management processes. Procedural controls are the defined rules for conducting day-to-day business activities.

Implementing a layered approach to information security is recommended when protecting critical assets and information. A layered approach means that the organization implements a combination of two or more security controls when protecting critical assets and information. Implementing a layered approach is one of the best defensive strategies for protecting critical company data and assets.

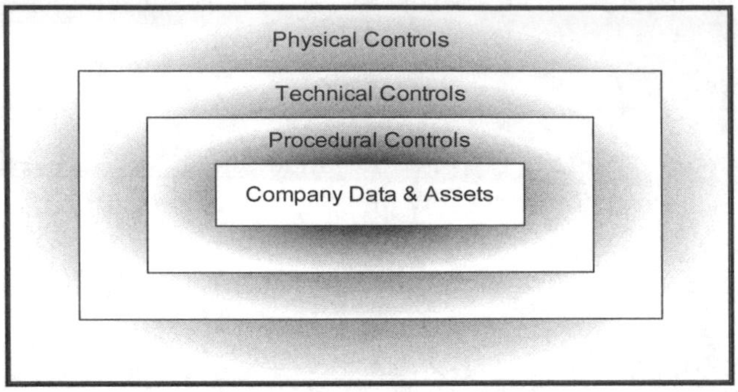

Figure: 14-1:

Preventive, Detective and Corrective Controls

When dealing with specific threats or incidents, specific security controls are needed. The three controls specifically identified by ITIL are Prevention/Reduction, Detection/Repression, and Correction/Recovery.

- **Prevention and Reduction controls** – are put in place in advance, and are designed to reduce the likelihood of potential incidents. They can range from allocation and control of access rights, to the implementation of cryptographic controls, and from carrying out regular data and software backups, to the development and testing of IT service continuity plans.
- **Detection and Repression controls** – are associated with the handling of actual security incidents and minimizing negative business impacts. They include monitoring, using event alert systems, virus checking, and blocking of user accounts after a pre-defined number of failed access attempts.
- **Correction and Recovery controls** – come into force when all other controls have failed. They are concerned with restoring data and software backups as quickly as possible, or with implementing other fall-back techniques.

Information Security Model

The only truly secure system is one that is powered off, cast in a block of concrete and sealed in a lead-lined room with armed guards.
– Gene Spafford

Policy

Achieving the level of security set forth in the security policy requires the support of executive management. The security policy document identifies a set of mandatory management and employee guidelines and contains at a minimum the:

- Objectives and scope of information security for the organization.
- Information security goals and management principles.
- Definitions of information security roles and responsibilities.
- Relationships between specific security policies and guidelines.

Within an organization, factors that result from laws and regulations drive policy. Great examples of regulations that impact security policy include the US regulations, Health Insurance Portability and Accountability Act (HIPAA), and Sarbanes-Oxley (SOX). HIPAA is primarily used to ensure that key information such as individual health information is protected through the adoption of privacy and security standards. Section 404 of the Sarbanes Oxley Act makes it mandatory to explicitly take responsibility for establishing and maintaining an adequate internal control structure for protecting critical assets and information within a public organization.

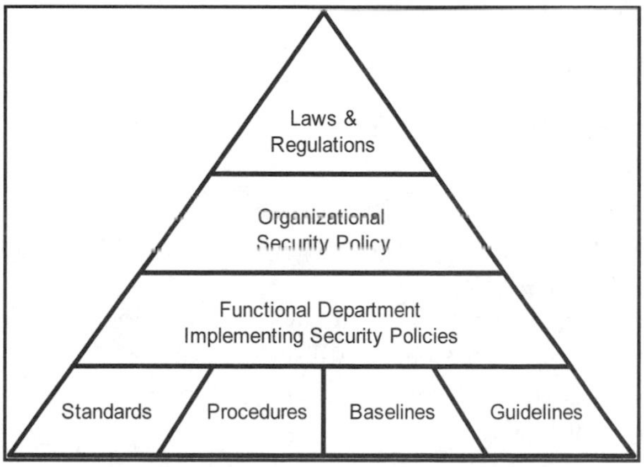

Figure: 14-2: Policy pyramid

Security Policy Supporting Items:

- **Standards** – are the rules specifying how hardware and software is to be used and specifying expected behavior of employees. An example is that employees should not use business equipment for personal activities.
- **Baselines** – identify the minimum level of security required within an organization. An example is that all desktop computers must have the current service pack and firewall software installed and enabled.
- **Procedures** – provide documentation of the exact actions required to achieve a specific outcome. An example is the checklist used by Service Desk staff to appropriately route calls.
- **Guidelines** – are recommended actions and guides for users to follow where standards do not apply. An example of a recommendation is that all employees take computer security awareness training every six months.

Roles and Responsibilities

It is very important that individual roles, responsibilities, and authority be clearly defined, communicated, and understood by all employees within the organization. Following are roles that may be identified:

- **Executive management** – holds the highest level of responsibility for the security of information.
- **Information system security professionals** – are responsible for design, implementation, management, and review of a company's security policy, measures, standards, practices and procedures, baselines and guidelines.
- **Data owners** – are responsible for determining the classification levels or sensitivity of data as well as the integrity and maintenance of data. Data owners are usually members of senior/executive management.
- **Data custodian -** is responsible for maintenance and protection of data. This includes performing backups, keeping systems updated, installing operating systems, validating the integrity of data, and ensuring that the objectives in the company's security policy, standards, and guidelines are being followed.
- **Technology providers -** assist in the implementation of information security.
- **Process owners -** ensure that consistent processes are in place and aligned with the company's security policy.
- **Users** – are responsible for following the procedures documented in the company's security policy.
- **Information system auditors** – are responsible for providing an independent assessment to management with regards to whether the security policy, standards, procedures, control measures, and practices comply with the company's security objectives.

Risk Analysis

Risk analysis involves doing a thorough analysis of identified risks to determine how they might impact the business. Risk analysis is an essential step to understanding costs and impacts involved in managing risks that could occur within the business. There are at least six steps involved in Risk analysis:

1. Understand the goal and scope of analysis.
2. Estimate and assign values to assets that need protection.
3. Identify each threat, vulnerability, and the threat agents.
4. Estimate the full loss potential of each risk.
5. Estimate the probability and frequency of a risk becoming reality.
6. Suggest countermeasures and remedial measures that are cost-effective and can be implemented to mitigate risks.

Quantitative Risk Analysis – focuses on analyzing the numeric probability of each risk and its consequences to the overall organization.

Qualitative Risk Analysis – focuses on assessing the impact and likelihood of identified risks. This process prioritizes risks according to the potential impact to the organization.

Planning and Implementation

Security is a complicated process that affects all areas of IT. As such, it is important to ensure proper planning if implementation is to be effective and the potential of risk is to be mitigated, or occurrences of risk are to be appropriately managed.

Operation

Operation determines how security controls are managed and monitored on an on-going basis. It includes processes and procedures for addressing specific security incidents.

Evaluation and Audit

Evaluation and Audit determines how the effectiveness of security controls is to be assured and improved on over time.

The IT Security Process

The mantra of any good security engineer is: 'Security is a not a product, but a process.' It's more than designing strong cryptography into a system; it's designing the entire system such that all security measures, including cryptography, work together.
— Bruce Schneier

The IT security management process model provides an overview of the IT security management process. It includes the six activities (sub-processes) of planning, implementing, evaluating, maintaining, controlling, and reporting. These activities are graphically in Figure 14-3.

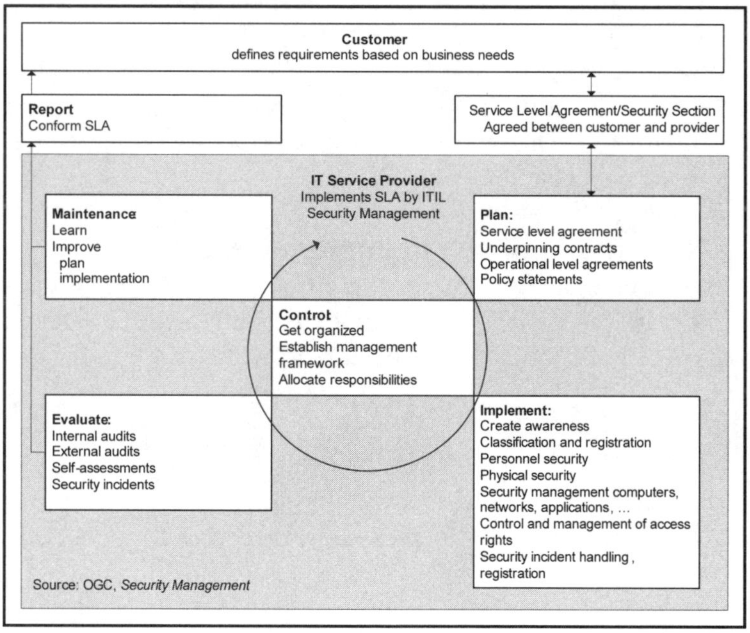

Figure: 14-3: Security Management process model

Planning

Wisdom consists in being able to distinguish among dangers and make a choice of the least harmful.
– Niccolo Machiavelli

Planning begins with the policy directives and translates those directives into the specific actions needed to ensure security. There are four documents to which security planning efforts are focused. Security is spelled out in broad terms inside service level agreements. More detailed requirements are documented in operational level agreements. Where underpinning contracts are in place, security arrangements are documented for third-party suppliers in those contracts. Finally, there are security handbooks, which provide detailed operational level security guidance for processes and procedures.

Security Section in SLAs

Service security is concerned with confidentiality, integrity, and availability (CIA) of critical assets and data. Requirements for CIA in any given service are spelled out in the security section of the SLA.

The Security Plan

As with all projects, there is a planning document that details all the requirements of a successful project. The Security Plan documents the broad security requirements and the efforts needed to implement those requirements.

Implementing

Those who do not archive the past are condemned to retype it!
– Garfinkel and Spafford

Implementing involves a wide range of security controls, as defined in the plan. It covers areas such as:

- Asset classification and control.
- Personnel security.
- Communications and operations management.
- Access control.

All organizations differ in their security needs. These needs depend on many factors, such as the industry, government interaction, uniqueness of product, etc.

Even so, every organization needs to apply basic principles to manage risk. For instance, every organization needs to have a formal change management process to manage changes to security and to understand where changes in the infrastructure require adjustments to security.

Objectives:

- Ensure that there is an approach for the implementation of security controls and for maintaining the protection of the organization's assets.
- Promote security by maintaining the required level of knowledge and experience of all employees, thus promoting security and assisting in the reduction of the risks that may arise from both intentional and unintentional human actions.
- Ensure that all IT resources are used properly, correctly, and securely.
- Prevent unauthorized access to information and information systems in order to:
    - Protect the confidentiality of the information.
    - Prevent unauthorized and undesirable changes.
    - Prevent damage or destruction of information or software.
    - Prevent disruption of the normal production processes.

Evaluating

But it doesn't have to be this way. We can do things better. We need to stop doing business as usual and start focusing on end-to-end quality. Security needs to be built in from the start -- not slapped on after the fact.
– Gene Spafford

There are three types of evaluation recognized by ITIL:

1. Self-assessments
2. Internal audits
3. External audits

Organizations should conduct self-assessments to understand what their strengths and weaknesses are in terms of security. This information can be used as the basis of a security improvement plan. Internal audits are conducted within organizations by internal but independent bodies specifically tasked with auditing responsibilities. This is a more formal aspect of self-assessment, usually directed from the policy level. Further external audits, performed by third parties, serve to provide an objective examination of strengths and weaknesses for use in corporate governance and assurance of third parties.

Objective:

- Supervise and check compliance with the security policy of the organization, agreed upon security standards, and the SLA security sections.

Maintaining

The methods that will most effectively minimize the ability of intruders to compromise information security are comprehensive user training and education. Enacting policies and procedures simply won't suffice. Even with oversight the policies and procedures may not be effective: my access to Motorola, Nokia, ATT, Sun depended upon the willingness of people to bypass policies and procedures that were in place for years before I compromised them successfully.
– Kevin Mitnick

As with everything in IT, security requirements change constantly. Security threats come and go and the IT infrastructure is constantly changing and introducing new and different security concerns. It is important that maintenance activities are managed so that they keep up with the changing needs for security.

Objectives:

- To deliver agreed upon levels of security and to improve them when required
- To improve implementation of specified security controls

Controlling

Amateurs hack systems, professionals hack people.
– Bruce Schneier

The control activity sets the parameters in which IT security management operates, and it ensures that the security management activities achieve their stated objectives.

The control activity defines the sub-processes of security management and all functions, roles, and responsibilities within them. It also details any organizational considerations.

Objectives:

- Manage information security in order to facilitate secure operation by the IT service provider.
- Establish a management framework to initiate and manage information security in the organization.
- Establish an organizational structure to prepare, approve, and implement the information security policy and to allocate responsibilities and implement the security controls.

Reporting

A better understanding of trade-offs leads to a better understanding of security, and consequently to more sensible security decisions.
– Bruce Schneier

Reporting is essential for providing supporting information for allocation of scarce resources to security activities. It includes maintaining a security incident database so that assertions and requests for resources can be supported.

Objective:

- Provide relevant information on information security.

Conclusion

IT Security Management is concerned with implementing the security policy that is directed by executive management. IT does not create the security policy, it provides information in support of its development. It is concerned with both internal and external security primarily in the areas of confidentiality, integrity, and availability. It utilizes four distinct forms of controls: organizational, physical, technical, and procedural. There are four specific documents utilized in Security Management planning: SLAs, OLAs, UCs, and security handbooks. The security plan organizes all of the Security Management activities. Finally, controls are ensured by auditing and reporting. The three types of auditing are; self-assessment, internal audits, and external audits.

Exam Preparation Questions

1. What four things does IT Security Management enable and ensure?
2. Whose responsibility is security policy?
3. What is the job of IT Security Management?
4. What are the two dimensions in which information can be supplied and secured?
5. What three concepts are the foundation of information value?
6. What are the four forms of security controls?
7. What are the three specifically identified security controls?
8. What are the four things that every security policy should contain?
9. What are the six activities of the IT security process?
10. What are the four documents upon which security planning is focused?
11. What does the security plan document?
12. List two objectives of the implementation activity.
13. What are the three types of evaluation?
14. What is the objective of the evaluating activity?
15. What are the objectives of the maintaining activity?
16. What are the three objectives of the controlling activity?
17. What is the objective of the reporting activity?
18. Be able to define the following in ITIL terms:
    1. IT Security Management
    2. CIA

Appendix A

Basic Availability

$$Availability\% = \left(\frac{(AST - DT)}{AST} \times 100\right)$$

DT is the three hours of unplanned downtime

$$AST = ((24hrs \times 7days) - 2hrsPlannedMaintenance)$$

AST = 166

$$Availability\% = \left(\frac{(166 - 3)}{166} \times 100\right)$$

Availability = **98.19%**

End-User Perspective

$$EUA\% = \left(\frac{(EUPT - EUDT)}{EUPT} \times 100\right)$$

$$AST = ((24 \times 7) - 2)$$

AST = 166

$$EUPT = (166 \times 1000)$$

EUPT = 166,000 hours or 9,960,000 minutes

$$EUDT = ((60 \times 50) + (25 \times 20) + (125 \times 1000) + (20 \times 1))$$

EUDT = 128,520 minutes

$$EUA\% = \left(\frac{(9,960,000 - 128,520)}{9,960,000} \times 100\right)$$

EUA = **98.7%**

Total Infrastructure Availability

$$ServiceAvailability\% = (Comp1 \times Comp2 \times Comp3 \times Comp4) \times 100$$

$$ServiceAvailability\% = (0.98 \times 0.98 \times 0.975 \times 0.96) \times 100$$

Service Availability = **89.89%**

Appendix B

Type of Incident	Main Category	Sub-Category	Indication Priority
Failure	Software	Word processing	2
		Spreadsheet	2
		Business Application	1
	Hardware	Mainframe	1
		Midrange	1
		Server	1
		Workstation	2
	Etc…		
Service Request	Password reset		1
	Change toner cartridge		3
	Help User	Office software	3
		Business Application	2

Indication priority is an initial priority recommendation that can be further refined based on impact and urgency

Figure -1: Classification coding system

		Impact		
		High	Medium	Low
Urgency	High	1	2	3
	Medium	2	3	4
	Low	3	4	5

Figure -2: Priority coding system

Priority Code	Description	Target Resolution Time
1	Critical	1 hour
2	High	8 hours
3	Medium	24 hours
4	Low	48 hours
5	Planning	Planned

Figure -3: Priority code key

Glossary of Terms

Abbreviations and Acronyms

ABC	Activity Based Costing
BCM	Business Continuity Management
CAB	Change Advisory Board
CAB/EC	Change Advisory Board / Executive Committee
CCTA	Central Computer and telecommunications Agency
CDB	Capacity Management Database
CFIA	Component Failure Impact Analysis
CI	Configuration Item
CIA	Confidentiality, Integrity, Availability
CMDB	Configuration Management Data Base
CMM	Capability Maturity Model
COBIT	Control Objectives for IT and Related Technologies
CSF	Critical Success Factor
DHS	Definitive Hardware Store
DSL	Definitive Software Library
EFQM	European Foundation for Quality Management
EXIN	Netherlands Examination Institute for Information Technology
FSC	Forward Schedule of Change

FTA	Fault Tree Analysis
HIPAA	Health Insurance Portability and Accountability Act of 1996 (US)
ICMB	International ITIL Certification Management Board
IPMA	International Project Management Association
ISEB	Information System Examination Board
ISO	International Standards Organization
IT	Information Technology
ITAMM	IT Availability Metrics Model
ITIL	Information Technology Infrastructure Library
ITSCM	IT Service Continuity Management
ITSM	Information Technology Service Management
KB	Knowledge Base
KE	Known-Error
KPI	Key Performance Indicator
MOF	Microsoft Operations Framework
MSF	Microsoft Solutions Framework
MTBF	Mean Time Between Failures
MTBSI	Mean Time Between Systems Incidents
MTTR	Mean Time To Repair
OGC	Office of Government Commerce
OLA	Operational Level Agreement
PDCA	Plan, Do, Check, Act
PIR	Post Implementation Review

PMI	Project Management Institute
PSA	Projected Service Availability
RFC	Request for Change
ROI	Return On Investment
SD	Service Desk
SIP	Service Improvement Program
SLA	Service Level Agreement
SLAM	Service Level Agreement Monitoring
SLM	Service Level Management
SLR	Service Level Requirement
SOX	Sarbanes-Oxley Legislation (US)
TCO	Total Cost of Ownership
TQM	Total Quality Management
UC	Underpinning Contract

Terms

Absorbed indirect costs	Costs that are easily divided, such as floor space. Since it can be easily divided, there is rarely any dispute about which budget the money should come from.
Attribute	A descriptive characteristic of a configuration item, such as a make/model number, version number, supplier, purchase contract number, release number, data format, role or relationship, held in the CMDB.
Availability	The ability of an IT service or component to perform its required function at a stated time or over a stated period of time.
Baseline	A snapshot or a position, which is recorded. Although the position may be updated later, the baseline remains unchanged and available as a reference of the original state and as a comparison against the current position (PRINCE2.)
Build	The final stage in producing a usable configuration. The process involves taking one or more input *Configuration Items* and processing them (building them) to create one or more output Configuration Items, e.g., software compile and load.
Business critical calendar	identifies periods of time when even minor changes can have major business impact (the classic example is end-of-month for accounting systems.)
Business function	A business unit within an organization, e.g., a department, division, branch.
Business process	A group of business activities, undertaken by an organization in pursuit of a common goal.
Capacity	the maximum power, performance, content or output of a system or component.

Change
1. Any deliberate action that alters the form, fit, or function of configuration items – typically, an addition, modification, movement, or deletion that impacts the IT infrastructure.

2. The addition, modification or removal of approved, supported, or baselined hardware, network, software, application, environment, system, desktop build or associated documentation.

Classification
The process of identifying the reason for an incident and the corresponding resolution action.

Configuration item (CI)
Component of an infrastructure – or an item, such as a Request for Change, associated with an infrastructure – which is (or is to be) under the control of Configuration Management.

Configuration management
The process of planning for, identifying, controlling and verifying the configuration items within a service.

Configuration management database (CMDB)
A database which contains all relevant details of each CI and the details of the important relationships between CIs.

Configuration structure
A hierarchy of all the CIs that comprise a configuration.

Contingency planning
Planning to address unwanted occurrences that may happen at a later time. Traditionally, the term has been used to refer to planning for the recovery of IT systems rather than entire business processes.

Continuous availability
A characteristic of the IT service that minimizes or masks the effects of all failures and planned downtime to the user.

Continuous operation
A characteristic of the IT service that minimizes or masks the effects of planned downtime to the user.

Counter measure	A check or restraint on the service designed to enhance security by reducing the risk of an attack (by reducing either the threat or the vulnerability), reducing the impact of an attack, detecting the occurrence of an attack and/or assisting in the recovery from an attack.
Critical success factor (CSF)	A measure of success or maturity of a project or process. It can be a state, a deliverable, or a milestone.
Definitive hardware store (DHS)	A physical location where replacement hardware can be stored for use to replace defective equipment in urgent situations.
Definitive software library (DSL)	A physical library, where all quality-controlled versions of all software configuration items (CIs) are held in their definitive form, together with any associated CIs such as license and other documentation.
Direct costs	Costs which can be allocated in full to a product, service, customer, cost center, or business activity.
Disaster	An event affecting a service or system such that significant effort is required to restore the original performance level.
Downtime	Total period that a service or component is not operational within agreed upon service times.
Error in infrastructure (Failure)	is when a functional unit is no longer fit for purpose.
Escalation	is passing information and/or requesting action on an incident, problem, or change to more senior staff (hierarchical) or other specialists (functional.)
Fault	is a condition that causes a functional unit to fail to perform the required function.

Forward schedule of changes (FSC) contains details of all the changes approved for implementation and their proposed implementation dates.

Functional escalation involves transferring an incident from one level of support to another, normally because of a lack of knowledge, lack of expertise, or a pre-determined period of time has elapsed.

Hierarchical escalation involves raising awareness of the incident to higher levels of management, such as when SLA breaches are likely to occur.

High availability A characteristic of the IT service that minimizes or masks the effects of IT component failure to the user

Impact A measure of the effect that an incident, problem, or change is having or might have on the business. It is often equal to the extent to which agreed or expected levels of service may be distorted. It also indicates the degree to which an incident departs from normal levels of service.

Impact analysis The identification of critical business processes, and the potential damage or loss that may be caused to the organization resulting from a disruption to those processes.

Incident Any event which is not part of the standard operation of a service, and which causes or may cause an interruption to, or a reduction in the quality of that service.

Incident control The process of identifying, recording, classifying, and progressing incidents until affected services return to normal operation.

Indirect costs Those costs incurred by more than one customer or service (sometimes called overhead.)

IT service A described set of facilities, IT and non-IT, supported by the IT Service Provider that fulfils one or more needs of the customer and that is perceived by the customer as a coherent whole.

Key performance indicator	A measurable quantity against which specific Performance Criteria can be set when drawing up the SLA.
Known-error	is a problem that is successfully diagnosed and for which a work-around is known. A known error may be a record in a known error database that is separate from the problem database. It may also be a status for an existing problem record within the problem database.
Maintainability	The ability of a component to be retained in or restored to an operational state.
Operational level agreement (OLA)	An internal agreement, covering the delivery of services which support the IT organizations in their delivery of services.
PD0005	Alternative title for the BSI publication "A Code of Practice for IT Service Management."
Priority	The value given to an incident, problem, or change to indicate its relative importance in order to ensure the appropriate allocation of resources, and to determine the timeframe within which action is required.
Problem	is the unknown underlying cause of one or more incidents.
Process	A connected series of actions, activities, changes, etc., performed by agents with the intent of satisfying a purpose or achieving a goal.
Release	A collection of new and/or changed CIs, which are tested and introduced into the live environment together.
Release unit	The portion of the IT infrastructure that is normally released together.
Reliability	Freedom from operational failure.
Request for change (RFC)	Form, or screen, used to record details of a request for a change to any CI within an infrastructure or to procedures and items associated with the infrastructure.

Risk	A measure of the exposure to which an organization may be subjected. This is a combination of the likelihood of a business disruption occurring and the possible loss that may result from such business disruption.
Risk analysis	The identification and assessment of the level (measure) of the risks calculated from the assessed values of assets and the assessed levels of threats to, and vulnerabilities of, those assets.
Role	A set of responsibilities, activities, and authorizations.
Roll-out	Delivering, installing, and commissioning an integrated set of new or changed CIs across logical or physical parts of an organization
Service	One or more IT systems which enable a business process.
Service catalogue	Written statements of IT services, default levels, and options.
Service request	Every incident not being a failure in the IT Infrastructure.
Single points of failure (SPOF)	Components in the service chain, where a component failure will cause a service failure.
Structural resolution	occurs when a change has been implemented to resolve the root cause of an error in the infrastructure.
Super-user	In some organizations it is common to use 'expert' users (commonly known as super or expert users) to deal with first line support problems and queries. This is typically in specific application areas, or geographical locations, where there is no requirement for full-time support staff. This valuable resource, however, needs to be carefully coordinated and utilized.
Threat	An indication of an unwanted incident that could impinge on the system in some way. Threats may be deliberate (e.g., willful damage) or accidental (e.g., operator error).

Transfer costs Costs transferred from other parts of the organization.

Unabsorbed indirect costs Costs that are not easily divided, such as insurance, electricity, or facilities maintenance. These are costs incurred by multiple departments that have to be recovered from the different departments' budgets in an acceptable way (sometimes referred to as uplift.)

Urgency A measure of business criticality of an incident, problem, or change, where there is an effect upon business deadlines. Urgency reflects the time available for repair or avoidance before the impact is felt by the business.

Variant A CI that, although different in some small way, has the same basic functionality as other CIs, and therefore may be required to be analyzed along with its generic group.

Version An identified instance of a Configuration Item within a product breakdown structure or Configuration Structure for the purpose of tracking and auditing change history. Also used for Software Configuration Items to define a specific identification released in development for drafting, review or modification, test or production.

Vulnerability A weakness of the system and its assets, which could be exploited by threats.

Work-around Method of avoiding an incident or problem, either from a temporary fix or from a technique that means the customer is not reliant on a particular aspect of the service that is known to have a problem.

Bibliography

Berkhout, Michiel; Roy Harrow; Brian Johnson; Shirley Lacy; Vernon Lloyd; Don Page; Marc van Goethem; Hans van den Bent; Gus Welter; *Best Practice for Service Support,* Third Impression, Published by The Stationery Office (TSO) for the Office of Government Commerce under licence from the controller of Her Majesty's Stationery Office, United Kingdom, 2001.

Bartlett, John; David Hinley; Brian Johnson; David Johnston; Chris Keeling; Vernon Lloyd; Ian MacDonald; John Mather; Gerry McLaughlin; Colin Rudd; David Wheeldon; and Rob Young, *Best Practice for Service Delivery,* Third Impression, Published by The Stationery Office (TSO) for the Office of Government Commerce under licence from the controller of Her Majesty's Stationery Office, United Kingdom, 2001.

Cazemier, Jacques, and Dr. Ir. Paul L. Overbeck, and Drs. Louk M.C. Peters, *Best Practice for Security Management,* Seventh Impression, Published by The Stationery Office (TSO) for the Office of Government Commerce under licence from the controller of Her Majesty's Stationery Office, United Kingdom, 2001.

Evans, Ivor, and Ivor Macfarlane, *A dictionary of IT Service Management, Terms, Acronyms and Abbreviations*, itSMF Ltd., United Kingdom, 2001.

Macfarlane, Ivor, and Colin Rudd, *IT Service Management: A companion to the IT Infrastructure Library*, Version Two, itSMF Ltd., United Kingdom, 2001.

Cambray, Derek, and Gary Hodgkiss, *IT Security Management*, Version 1.0, itSMF Ltd., United Kingdom, 2003

Liker, Jeffrey K., *The Toyota Way: 14 Management Principles From the Worlds Greatest Manufacturer, McGraw Hill, New Yourk, New York, 2004, ISBN 0-07-139231-9*

International Trade Administration/US Depart. of Commerce, Automobile Net Income Data charts, <**http://www.ita.doc.gov/td/auto/finwebjan2004prelim.pdf**>**, accessed on December 2004.**

1000Ventures.com, Kaizen quote, <**http://www.1000ventures.com**

/business_guide/glossary_lean_kaizen.html>, accessed on December 2004.

Bond (Ed), J.van, *IT Service Management: an introduction based on ITIL,* Second Edition, Van Haren Publishing, Zaltbommel, The Netherlands, 2004

"IT Doesn't Matter," *The Harvard Business Review*, Vol. 81, Issue 5, May 2003, p. 41

BusinessTrainingWorks.com, general quotes, <http://www.businesstrainingworks.com/customer_service_quotations.htm>, **accessed on** June 25, 2005.

Thinkexist.com, Quotes, <http://en.thinkexist.com/quotation/information_is_a_source_of_learning-but_unless_it/226524.html>, **accessed on** June 25, 2005.

Bartleby.com, Quotes, <http://www.bartleby.com/100/>, **accessed on** June 25, 2005.

Answers

Chapter 7 Answers

Chapter 8 Answers

Chapter 9 Answers

Chapter 10 Answers

Chapter 11 Answers

Chapter 12 Answers

Chapter 13 Answers

Chapter 14 Answers

Index

F

G

H

I

K

L

M

Q

R

S

W

13526458554